The Essentials of
POWER,
INFLUENCE, *and*
PERSUASION

The Business Literacy for HR Professionals Series

The Business Literacy for HR Professionals Series educates human resource professionals in the principles, practices, and processes of business and management. Developed in conjunction with the Society for Human Resource Management, these books provide a comprehensive overview of the concepts, skills, and tools HR professionals need to be influential partners in developing and executing organizational strategy. Drawing on rich content from Harvard Business School Publishing and the Society for Human Resource Management, each volume is closely reviewed by a content expert as well as senior HR professionals. Whether you are aspiring to the executive level in your organization or already in a leadership position, these authoritative books provide the basic business knowledge you need to play a strategic role.

Other books in the series:

The Essentials of Finance and Budgeting
The Essentials of Managing Change and Transition
The Essentials of Negotiation
The Essentials of Corporate Communications and Public Relations

The Essentials of POWER, INFLUENCE, *and* PERSUASION

Harvard Business School Press
Boston, Massachusetts

and

the Society for Human Resource Management
Alexandria, Virginia

Library of Congress Cataloging-in-Publication Data

The essentials of power, influence, and persuasion.
    p. cm. — (Business literacy for HR professionals) (The business literacy
                    for HR professionals series)
        Includes bibliographical references and index.
                    ISBN 1-59139-821-5
    1. Personnel management—Psychological aspects. 2. Executive ability. I. Society
for Human Resource Management (U.S.) II. Harvard business literacy for HR
                        professionals series.
                    HF5549.E7976 2006
                    658.3001'9—dc22
                        2006007135

Contents

Introduction

Three executives and their CEO were sitting around a conference table. They were conferring about a matter of importance to them and to most other full-time employees of their four-hundred-person company: how much money would be put into the bonus pool for distribution this year?

Each person at the table had something to say about the matter. Cheryl, the human resources vice president, understood the details of the bonus system and its impact on employees more than anyone. She argued strenuously for a generous payout, citing the company's strong financial condition and the meager bonus paid the previous year. "People have worked exceptionally hard this year," she said, "and they are expecting to be rewarded in an exceptional way. They've earned it." Cheryl went on to describe how the bonus amount she favored fit in with the company's total compensation and benefits package, and she compared that package to those of other employers in the area. George, the chief operating officer, nodded in agreement and offered supporting comments.

LaNita, the chief financial officer, who had her thumb on current and projected spending activities, sounded a more cautious note and argued for a slightly smaller deal. She had substantial influence over Chan, the CEO, on money matters—so much so that she could trump the wishes of her fellow executives.

These four individuals eventually reached a decision that no other employees were empowered to make. The CEO transmitted that decision to the board of directors for final approval. Only the board could authorize the bonus expenditure. But the board was likely to approve the decision because of Chan's influence over them. Board members viewed the CEO as credible, effective, and trustworthy. If Chan said that $1.8 million for the bonus pool was the right number, most board members would accept his judgment, especially if that number was in line with current company performance and future plans. If there were holdouts, the CEO would try to persuade them that his decision was sound. He would cite the endorsements of Cheryl, the vice president of HR; as well as those of LaNita, the CFO; and George, the COO—each of whom would be on hand to back up the boss at the board meeting. Chan would also explain the systematic method used to determine the $1.8 million payout and describe how those bonus funds would motivate employees without jeopardizing pending plans.

Though fabricated, this short tale accurately represents how decisions get made and initiatives get supported in business organizations. And it illustrates the three related ideas explored in this book: power, influence, and persuasion. In this story each of the four executives had influence on the amount of the bonus payout—some more than others. Persuasion was applied where unanimity was absent. Chan, the CEO, exercised his power in making the bonus payout decision, and the board exercised its power in approving it.

Power, influence, and persuasion have always existed in social systems. One of the more striking examples is found in France's Louis XIV, a seventeenth-century monarch who claimed his power by divine right. Louis considered his power absolute, but he was open to influence by his ministers, seemingly without recognizing it. For instance, he leaned heavily on Jean Baptiste Colbert for financial advice, and he looked to the Marquis de Louvois for military strategy. Although Louis made it clear that he would not share authority with any of his ministers, he could not rule without them. Nor could he conceal from them his major personal weakness: an unquenchable fondness for flattery. This weakness provided the channel through which ministers, mistresses, and courtiers influenced him and persuaded him to do what they wanted. Louvois, for example, used the king's love of praise to steer him into wars he would not otherwise have entered. According to one contemporary, the duke de Saint Simon, Louvois "persuaded [the king] that he had greater talents for war than any of his generals." Thus, even a holder of absolute power is susceptible to influence and persuasion by others, as you will see in this book.

Today's businesses are a far cry from the regime of Louis XIV. Power is no longer absolute but instead is divided among managers, executives, directors, and shareholders. Statutes limit the power of companies and their managers over employees. Formal authority still exists, but the role of influence and persuasion has grown increasingly important.

But what exactly do we mean by these terms? We define *power* as the potential to allocate resources and to make and enforce decisions. For a manager, understanding how to obtain power and use it wisely

L'Eminence Grise

More than a few powerful leaders have been heavily influenced by others. Perhaps one of the most successful and effective of these influencers was Cardinal Richelieu (1585–1642), adviser and ultimately prime minister to Louis XIII. Contemporaries gave him the nickname *eminence rouge* (the red eminence) because of his red clerical garb. A determined advocate of royal power and the bane of anyone who challenged it, Richelieu famously said, "If you give me six lines written by the most honest man, I will find something in them to hang him."

Today many use the term *eminence grise* (the gray, or shadowy, eminence) to refer to anyone who rules from behind the throne or who has unusual power over the formal holder of authority. Eminence grise originally referred to Père Joseph, a French cleric and secretary to Richelieu.

Does your organization have its own eminence grise? If so, who is it?

is an essential, though seldom recognized, skill. John Kotter, a professor of management at Harvard Business School, put it this way:

> *Most managerial jobs require one to be skilled at the acquisition and use of power . . . I suspect that a large number of managers—especially the young, well-educated ones—perform significantly below their potential because they do not understand the dynamics of power and because they have not nurtured and developed the instincts needed to effectively acquire and use power.*[1]

Influence is an extension of power; it is the mechanism through which you use power to change others' behavior or attitudes. Unlike power, however, influence can produce an effect without the apparent exertion of force, compulsion, or direct command. In a sense, it is power in a velvet glove. (Remember the classic Mafia movie line, "Make him an offer he can't refuse.") In some cases, influence is exerted through manipulation. Influence can also be exercised by people who have no formal power. Every manager must understand how to influence others: bosses, peers, and subordinates.

Persuasion is closely related to influence but is also very different. It isn't a force, and it has no coercive component. Instead, it is a process through which you aim to change or reinforce the attitudes, opinions, or behaviors of others. Anyone who becomes skilled in the art of persuasion enjoys an edge in selling his or her ideas or products or simply making things happen. Persuasion is an essential life skill, as useful at home as it is in the workplace.

Every business and virtually every human society operates with the help of power, influence, and persuasion. They are as essential to organizational and interpersonal functions as the air we breathe. Every one of us is routinely on the giving or receiving end of power, influence, and persuasion—often simultaneously. Even as we are subjected to the power of our bosses, we are influencing and persuading them. We also have similar relationships with our peers and subordinates.

This book will help you to understand these three concepts and discover why they're so important to HR professionals. As you'll see, savvy use of your power, influence, and persuasion can help you win the resources and cooperation you need to implement valuable HR initiatives and programs. These skills can also enable you to build your credibility and move forward in your career. But wielding your power, influence, and persuasion takes careful thought and a thorough understanding of how these mechanisms work in general and in your particular organization. In this book, you'll find a wealth of practical advice on how you can put them to work.

What You'll Find in This Book

In this volume, we deal with power, influence, and persuasion in that order. Chapter 1 lays the foundation by clarifying why power, influence, and persuasion matter to HR practitioners—including the importance of establishing your personal and professional credibility. Chapter 2 explains why power is necessary in organizations even though our society distrusts power and those who seek it. This chapter explains three managerial approaches to power and indicates which is best for you and your organization.

Where does power come from? Chapter 3 addresses that question. It discusses the characteristics of positional power, relational power, and personal power. It also describes constraints on these powers. For example, the power vested in a position in the organization is naturally limited by the power holder's dependence on others: peers, bosses, and subordinates. But even within these natural constraints, you can still enhance your power, and this chapter shows you how.

Real power is realized only through some form of expression, as described in chapter 4. Influence is one way that you can express your power so as to change, direct, or affect others' behavior. This chapter describes the limitations of direct power and explains how to apply your power indirectly to influence the outcomes you seek. To apply influence, however, you must open yourself to influence by others; it's a two-way street. This chapter offers practical suggestions for increasing your influence in your organization. Chapter 5 takes the matter of influence a step further by illustrating six specific tactics that you can use on the job—including maneuvering within your company's reporting hierarchy, leveraging invisible social networks, and helping new leaders assimilate into the organization.

Even people who possess formal power use persuasion as their primary means of changing others' behavior and affecting decisions. To persuade is to use argument or entreaty to get others to adopt a belief or particular behavior. Chapters 6 and 7 tackle the concept of persuasion. The first of these chapters explains the five elements of persuasion and discusses how various audiences and people with various decision styles are susceptible to different forms of persuasion. Chapter 7 shows you how to win your listeners' minds *and* hearts. It explains how to appeal to the logical side of your audience and then describes techniques for appealing to their emotional side. You'll find plentiful information on how word choice, vivid descriptions, metaphors, analogies, and stories can help your idea resonate with an audience.

Chapter 8 is about formal presentations, one of the most common opportunities for persuasion in modern business. If you make formal presentations regularly and would like them to be more effective, this chapter can help you. It suggests a presentation structure and a number of rhetorical devices perfected by the ancient Greeks. It also explains the various learning styles used by people and argues why you need to adapt your presentation style to them. In addition, you'll find helpful information about how to overcome presentation anxiety—a condition that can afflict even seasoned public speakers.

Most of us know the damage that power, influence, and persuasion can cause when handled carelessly, irresponsibly, or with malignant intent. Chapter 9 addresses the ethics problem, suggesting two standards to which power, influence, and persuasion must conform to be considered ethical. This chapter also takes things a step further, offering five ways by which you can help create an ethical culture within your organization.

In chapter 10, you'll find profiles of HR professionals who have successfully used their power, influence, and persuasion skills in various situations and with numerous constituencies. For example, some have applied these skills to start a new job in HR on the right foot or to forge positive relationships with "higher-ups." Others have used

their power, influence, and persuasiveness to motivate their direct reports, collaborate productively with peers, and win buy-in for strategic HR initiatives. Still others have applied their skills with particular
talent during tough times in their organizations. Their stories offer
valuable lessons for any HR practitioner.

Finally, chapter 11 helps you review the key principles and practices of power, influence, and persuasion. You'll also find a worksheet
that helps you develop a plan for further enhancing these skills. The
concluding section of this chapter offers suggestions for using your
power, influence, and persuasiveness to move forward in your career.

This book's content is based on a number of books, articles, and
online productions of Harvard Business School Publishing (HBSP)
and the Society for Human Resource Management (SHRM), including class notes, *Harvard Business Review* articles, the online learning
series Harvard ManageMentor®, *HR Magazine,* and SHRM surveys
and research reports.

When you've finished reading these chapters, you'll find several
helpful supplementary sections: a glossary of terms, four appendixes,
and a list of books and articles you may want to consult as you expand your knowledge of power, influence, and persuasion. The glossary contains terms we've italicized in the chapters. The appendixes
are as follows:

- Appendix A is a short piece entitled "Leading When You're
  Not the Boss." Many people find themselves in situations in
  which they are expected to lead but have no formal power to
  do so. Many team leaders, in fact, are outranked by team members. This appendix offers useful tips on how to act in this type
  of situation.

- Appendix B contains two forms that you may find useful when
  assessing an audience that you need to persuade and when assessing your own personal ability to persuade others. The first
  worksheet, "Assessing Your Audience," can also be found online
  at http://www.elearning.hbsp.org/businesstools. This worksheet

is one of many checklists, worksheets, and interactive tools available to readers without charge (within normal copyright restrictions) on the Harvard ManageMentor® Web site.

- Appendix C contains worksheets that help you identify your social network and assess its quality, as well as generate ideas for making the network more effective. For example, you'll identify ways to address overuse and underuse of certain individuals in your social network, as well as list the types of expertise to which you need access in your network.

- Appendix D explains how to make the most of presentation visuals. Almost everyone uses overheads or projected slides in their presentations to management or to their peers and subordinates. Visuals can get key points across and make them memorable. In the wrong hands, however, they can actually confuse or bore the audience, diminishing the impact of an entire presentation. This appendix offers commonsense rules for making the most of presentation visuals.

The Essentials of
POWER,
INFLUENCE, *and*
PERSUASION

CHAPTER ONE

Building Credibility as an HR Professional

Why Your Power, Influence, and Persuasion Skills Matter

Key Topics Covered in This Chapter

- *Prevailing perceptions of the HR profession*
- *The importance of personal credibility in exercising power, influence, and persuasiveness*
- *Strategies for establishing personal credibility*
- *The use of power, influence, and persuasion to overcome career obstacles*

HOW MUCH *credibility* do you have as an HR professional? That is, how well do you inspire others' belief in and acknowledgment of your expertise, abilities, and knowledge? And how much credibility does the HR profession have overall? As you'll see in this chapter, HR's credibility as a profession strongly affects its practitioners' personal credibility, as perceived by these professionals' superiors, peers, and the employees they serve. Personal credibility, in turn, determines the level of formal power an HR practitioner acquires, as well as the degree of influence and persuasiveness he or she exerts in the workplace. In a self-reinforcing cycle, effective use of power, influence, and persuasion further enhances one's personal credibility, which enables HR professionals to advance in their careers, seize new opportunities, and win promotions and salary increases. Personal credibility also allows HR practitioners to create more value for their organizations and to enhance their profession's credibility overall.

Let's take a closer look at these complex dynamics between professional and personal credibility, and their impact on your and other HR professionals' ability to exercise power, influence, and persuasion on the job.

How Credible Is HR?

According to one recently conducted survey of HR professionals, a profession's credibility, or professionalism, stems from several elements, including the following:[1]

- The profession's practitioners possess a body of knowledge and skills that others see as based on carefully thought out theories and requiring the exercise of considerable discretion.

- Practitioners require specific educational credentials for entry and career mobility.

- The profession controls a training program that produces the required credentials, and practitioners have access to schooling that is associated with higher learning.

- Practitioners view themselves (and are seen by others) as dedicated more to serving a higher good than to reaping economic rewards.

Given these criteria, what's the news regarding HR's credibility? According to this same study, the news is mixed. Let's consider the encouraging findings first. On one hand, many HR professionals report to the highest-level executives in their organizations—often the chief executive officer, chief financial officer, or chief operating officer. HR professionals positioned this high in their organization's reporting hierarchy possess a great degree of formal power—the potential to allocate resources as well as make and reinforce important decisions. This proximity to the most powerful individuals in their organizations also opens doors for these professionals to exercise their influence and persuasiveness. If you recall, influence is the mechanism through which you use your power to change others' behaviors and attitudes, and persuasion is the process you employ to sell your ideas to others.

There's additional good news: the responses to this survey suggest that about three-quarters of HR practitioners agree that society in general recognizes HR's body of knowledge and skills as a profession. In addition, managers, employees, and nonbusiness executives recognize that HR practitioners possess specific knowledge and skills that add value to their organizations.

Now for the not-so-encouraging news: fewer than half of the HR professionals who responded to this survey felt that the leaders of the senior management group in their organizations regarded them as true business partners. Indeed, of those who reported that they had encountered major obstacles in advancing in their HR career, most believed that their biggest obstacle was that HR "is not held in high esteem." This is a troubling finding, given that the majority of respondents agree that their career advancement in their organizations is determined largely by both HR executives and non-HR executives.

The inescapable conclusion? Though HR has credibility in some respects (particularly the body of knowledge and credentials associated with the field), it could use more of this essential quality in other respects, especially in the esteem in which others hold HR practitioners and the profession overall. The more HR can meet such criteria, the higher a degree of professionalism it will reach—further enhancing its practitioners' personal credibility. Happily, many HR professionals already possess extensive formal power by dint of their position in their organizations' reporting hierarchy. But judging from the survey respondents' answers, HR professionals can do more to strengthen their degree of influence and persuasiveness.

Why Is Credibility Important?

The credibility of the HR profession is vital for several reasons. For one thing, it translates into personal credibility for its practitioners. Specifically, it earns you the recognition of your internal and external customers, as well as society in general. Moreover, when these constituents perceive HR as credible, they feel greater respect for your and other HR professionals' work. Recognition and respect in turn lead to rewards—in the form of promotions and compensation, as well as greater autonomy and control over your work.

Thus, an HR professional's personal credibility constitutes a key HR competency: it enables you to exercise your formal power effectively, to influence those over whom you have no formal authority, and to persuade others to embrace and execute your ideas. It goes without saying that you benefit. But your organization benefits as well, because it extracts the full value of your human capital. By contrast, HR professionals who lack personal credibility risk being excluded from the strategic activities they need to accomplish in order to help their organizations succeed. Indeed, according to one expert, "For HR professionals, personal credibility is second only to strategic contribution when it comes to influencing business performance."[2]

Strategies for Establishing and Building Your Personal Credibility

How can you establish and build your personal credibility? Susan Meisinger, president and CEO of the Society for Human Resource Management, offers these suggestions:[3]

- Create a solid track record of delivering and accurately communicating measurable results for your organization.

- Follow through on commitments you've made, and act with integrity each step of the way.

- Cultivate positive, productive, and trust-based relationships with people inside and outside your organization—employees, line managers, executives, vendors, and customers.

- Quickly identify and resolve interpersonal problems that threaten your organization's productivity.

- Use words and actions to communicate key organizational and HR objectives. Every time you hire, promote, reward, or train employees, articulate the messages that will best engage and align them with critical organizational and HR goals.

Effective communication, reliable performance on the job, and a positive chemistry with colleagues are particularly potent ingredients for personal credibility. To that end, Wayne Brockbank and Dave Ulrich, professors at the University of Michigan Business School, offer these recommendations:[4]

- Strengthen your written and oral communication skills, so you can communicate effectively to large numbers of people in shorter time periods.

- Use both formal and informal communication channels to convey your messages.

- Ask important questions that help to frame complex ideas in useful ways.

- Strive for accuracy (lack of errors) in your work.

- Use empathy to address key constituents' concerns that are not directly work related.

- With key constituents, identify common interests that go beyond work boundaries.

- Discuss shared core values with key constituents.

See assessment tool 1-1 to gauge your personal credibility as an HR professional.

Assessment Tool 1-1
How Credible Are You?

For each of the following statements, circle the number that best describes how true the statement is with regard to what you do as an HR professional. "1" indicates never; "2," seldom; "3," some-times; "4," frequently; and "5," always.

1. I constantly seek to master new skills and acquire new knowledge.

    1   2   3   4   5

2. I cultivate trust-based relationships with superiors, peers, employees, vendors, customers, and other constituents.

    1   2   3   4   5

3. I emphasize shared values and common interests in my conversations with others.

1   2   3   4   5

4. I seek to broaden my experience as much as possible by participating in cross-functional teams and in professional associations.

1   2   3   4   5

5. I act with integrity, doing as I say and fulfilling commitments I've made.

1   2   3   4   5

6. I strive to accumulate a track record of measurable results for my company.

1   2   3   4   5

7. I use multiple communication channels to convey my company's goals to others.

1   2   3   4   5

8. I work constantly to reduce the errors made in my work.

1   2   3   4   5

9. I quickly identify and resolve interpersonal problems that threaten my organization's productivity.

1   2   3   4   5

10. I use empathy to address others' concerns.

1   2   3   4   5

Calculating Your Score

To calculate your score, add up the numbers you circled.

continued

Interpreting Your Score

The higher your score, the greater your personal credibility as an HR professional.

Score 40–50: You have established a solid foundation of personal credibility in your organization. You therefore probably find it relatively easy to exert your formal authority, as well as use influence and persuasion to make change happen.

Score 30–39: You've established some personal credibility in your organization. However, you could do more to strengthen your credibility.

Score 10–29: You would benefit from building and sustaining your personal credibility, so as to enhance your ability to exercise power, influence, and persuasion.

Using Your Credibility to Move Ahead in HR

A high degree of personal credibility enables you to exert your power, influence, and persuasion skills to move past career obstacles. One all-too-common obstacle to many HR professionals is a supervisor who doesn't support your ideas or your efforts to lead, motivate, and develop peers and employees. Chapter 2 describes various types of bosses and ways you can work most effectively with each type.

In addition to an unsupportive boss, HR professionals may encounter numerous other obstacles to moving forward in their careers. HR practitioners who responded to one recent survey listed roadblocks such as a lack of a clear HR career path; age, gender, or racial bias; shortage of opportunities to grow; a lack of business acumen; lack of a mentor; and a prohibitively small organization size. But as mentioned earlier, the most frequently cited career obstacle, in these respondents' opinion, is that HR is not held in high enough esteem.[5]

Fortunately, you can boost your chances of surmounting all of these obstacles by making savvy use of your personal credibility.

How? First, develop a comprehensive working knowledge of all aspects of HR administration—from hiring and compensation to benefits, safety, training, and legal issues. Second, develop a real depth of understanding and expertise in your own specialized area. Third, understand your organization, its business, its goals, and its particular challenges. Fourth, understand business in general. Learn the language and mechanics of business. Finally, acquire as broad a background and experience as you can.

Business writer Lin Grensing-Pophal advocates these strategies:[6]

- Ask to take on responsibilities in different areas within your company, or volunteer to serve on task forces or committees. If your organization offers few such opportunities, volunteer with local agencies and organizations that can help you widen your base of experience.

- Develop a clear understanding of your company's goals and ways in which the HR function can support those objectives. Move beyond a need or desire to "help and protect" employees and, instead, support the sometimes tough decisions that must be made (such as downsizing or terminations) to ensure the company's success. Help such decisions move forward as efficiently and effectively as possible.

- Hone your awareness of other areas of the company, the ways in which they function, and their unique needs and challenges. To sharpen this awareness, serve on committees and task forces comprising members of other departments.

- Network to gain information and benefit from others' expertise. Cultivate contacts by becoming active in local trade and industry groups, attending HR and industry-related conferences and conventions, and participating in online industry or trade forums.

- Constantly seek new opportunities to learn and grow—by taking classes, attending conferences or seminars, reading trade and professional journals, and staying up-to-date on the trends and issues affecting HR and the industry in which your company competes.

- Continually look for ways to improve the services you and your team offer the company. Can you streamline operations you're responsible for? Cut costs? Partner more effectively with internal customers to increase the value HR provides?

- Share your successes with your boss, peers, and higher-ups. Remind them of your achievements from time to time. This doesn't have to take the form of bragging: a simple e-mail or casual comment mentioning the results of a task force you're leading or pointing someone's attention to an article you found interesting will help ensure that influential people notice your successes.

- Let those around you know that you want more from your career than the position you currently hold. Ask them for their support, and get the word out through networking or through applying for career-enhancement opportunities or internal promotions.

- Behave as though you're already in the position you'd like to hold. Dress the part, and ensure that your personal demeanor and actions reflect those of someone who could command the position that interests you.

In addition to these techniques, workplace-trends researcher Dave Patel offers these ideas:[7]

- Whenever you identify a problem or issue that needs resolution, don't just criticize the current situation. Instead, offer constructive ideas for solving the problem.

- Deepen your political knowledge: gather information about the formal *and* informal power structures in your organization. Find out who gets listened to, who makes things happen, and to whom people go for resources and support.

- Accept that the responsibility for managing your career—through the use of planning, skills development, and mentoring relationships—lies with *you*.

See "HR in Action: Building and Leveraging Personal Credibility at General Electric" for a case study of one HR executive who has used his personal credibility to generate impressive results for his organization.

HR in Action: Building and Leveraging Personal Credibility at General Electric

As senior vice president of corporate human resources at General Electric, Bill Conaty has used numerous strategies to strengthen his personal credibility—and has generated remarkable value for his organization as a result. For example, he has continually sought opportunities to learn and grow. His rich and varied educational and professional background includes a bachelor's degree in business administration, a tour of military duty, and participation in a three-year managerial training program at GE. In addition, he has worked in human resource roles in many different GE divisions, including transportation and aerospace.

Conaty focuses his efforts on the company's strategic priorities. For instance, to support GE's goal of maintaining a pipeline of executive talent, he works hard to craft effective leadership-development programs, conduct ongoing reviews of top executives, and revise HR strategy so as to fulfill diversity needs. Thanks to such efforts, the process of selecting a successor to CEO Jack Welch unfolded smoothly, and GE was able to make the leadership transition without losing many second-tier executives.

Conaty's personal qualities have also earned him widespread respect and enhanced his ability to exercise his influence and drive strategic change. Peers extol his integrity and fairness, willingness to share credit and accept blame for failure, and ability to respect confidences and remain true to his own words. Such qualities have helped him successfully handle numerous union negotiations. "The unions trust him," Welch once said. "He's gotten a settlement in every single negotiation."

Conaty has won the trust of the nonunionized workforce as well, by shifting discussions about new business strategies to assessments of these strategies' potential impact on the workforce. By ensuring fairness in the company's dealings with employees and constantly communicating with workers about GE's thorniest issues, he has sold change initiatives to the workforce and

continued

helped GE carry out the structural shifts needed to remain competitive in its industry.

In addition, Conaty participates in numerous organizations to keep his finger on the pulse of business and ensure that his supervisors get the information they need to make key decisions. For example, he is chairman of the HR Policy Association and the National Academy of Human Resources, and he regularly attends activities and dinners sponsored by GE's affinity groups: the GE Women's Network, the African-American Forum, the Asian-Pacific Forum, and the Hispanic Network. This visible endorsement of the company's diversity goals, combined with the success of GE's diversity initiatives, has won GE honors from Catalyst, an organization working to advance women in business, and the Executive Leadership Council, a network of three hundred African American corporate executives in *Fortune* 500 companies.

Finally, Conaty stays in close contact with GE's top five hundred leaders, getting to know them personally, identifying development opportunities for them, and assessing their potential for higher-level positions. His open and candid relationships with them enable him to ensure that important information makes its way to these leaders. Executives feel comfortable confiding in him about their concerns. Thanks to his attention to leadership development and ability to cultivate trust-based relationships, GE enjoys an annual voluntary turnover among senior executives of just 3 percent—remarkable in a company whose executives are much sought after by other companies.

SOURCE: Anne Freedman, "Master of HR at GE," *Human Resource Executive,* October 16, 2004, 1, 16–23. Used with permission.

Clearly, building your credibility as an HR professional requires time, focus, and energy. But the results are well worth the effort. The greater your personal credibility, the greater your ability to exercise power, influence, and persuasion for the good of your company—which in turn further strengthens your credibility. You, your organization, and your profession all benefit.

Before moving on to chapter 2, take stock of your current understanding of power, influence, and persuasion by completing assessment tool 1-2.

Assessment Tool 1-2
Test Your Understanding of Power, Influence, and Persuasion

To gauge your understanding of the concepts in this book, take the following multiple-choice test. Then review the answer key that follows, which points you to particular chapters for more information on specific aspects of power, influence, and persuasion.

1. **Which of the following statements about power is false?**
   A. Power is the potential to allocate resources and make and enforce decisions.
   B. A manager's power is limited by his or her dependence on subordinates, superiors, and peers.
   C. The best use of a manager's power is to continually seek opportunities to enhance his or her department's power.
   D. A manager can change the style he or she uses to exert power.

2. **Which of the following is *not* a source of power?**
   A. A manager's position in the organizational hierarchy
   B. A manager's familiarity with his or her employees' job responsibilities
   C. A manager's relationships with others in his or her organization
   D. A manager's personal qualities, such as ability to articulate compelling goals

3. **What is influence?**
   A. The mechanism through which a manager uses his or her power to change others' behavior or attitudes
   B. The process by which a manager tries to sell his or her ideas to others
   C. The extension of a manager's persuasion skills
   D. The resources a manager possesses that he or she can trade with others to gain their collaboration

continued

4. **Which of the following is an example of how an HR executive can leverage invisible social networks?**
   A. Socialize after hours with important customers of his or her company
   B. Join professional associations related to the industry in which his or her company competes
   C. Ensure that his or her team has lunch together at least once a week
   D. Encourage managers to introduce their new employees to people outside their unit

5. **In exercising your persuasion skills, you need to consider the needs of influencers. Who are influencers?**
   A. They provide advice and information to key stakeholders and decision makers.
   B. They have the power to approve or reject your idea.
   C. They are the individuals who will be directly affected by the acceptance of your proposal.
   D. None of the above.

6. **You're developing a strategy to appeal to your audience's heart while giving a persuasive presentation. Which of the following strategies might you consider?**
   A. Discuss the forces driving the problem at hand, then show how your idea will eliminate the problem.
   B. Provide startling statistics and testimonials to back up your claims.
   C. Use compelling graphics to provide visual impact for your audience.
   D. Present an analogy that helps your audience relate your idea to one that's already familiar to them.

7. **You're preparing a presentation that you'll deliver to several of your company's key executives to gain approval for an HR program you're proposing. Which of the following presentation structures would you choose?**

A. Tell your audience what you're going to say, then present the information, and finally recap what you said.

B. Craft an introduction, a narrative, an argument for your idea, a refutation of your opponents' views, and a conclusion.

C. Start off with an appropriate joke or quip, present a compelling case for your idea, then tell a story revealing how someone benefited from implementing your idea.

D. Ask your listeners how familiar they are with the topic of your presentation, introduce some compelling statistics and facts illustrating the problem you're addressing, and then present your case.

8. **Which of the following is an example of unethical use of influence?**

A. A supervisor negotiating a pay raise with an employee tells the person that the departmental budget allows a 3 percent increase for each person in the group, and that if the person received a higher percentage increase, someone else in the group would have to accept a smaller raise. The budget has not in fact been structured as the supervisor describes.

B. An HR manager seeking to remove a poorly performing subordinate tells the person, "I hate to lose you, but that open position in the logistics department would help you get ahead in the company."

C. An executive who wants to recruit a talented associate to his team tells the person a falsehood: "Joining Maura's team instead of mine would be a poor career move for you. I've heard that Maura is planning to take early retirement this year, and once she's gone, her team will be rudderless."

D. All of the above.

9. **Which of the following statements is true about the abuse of power?**

continued

A. The number of incidents of fraudulent conduct in organizations has remained consistent over the past three decades.
B. HR professionals' abuse of their power can be particularly damaging in corporations.
C. HR professionals have more opportunities to abuse their power than other executives have.
D. Three of every four employee crimes is committed by an executive.

10. **To move forward in your career as an HR professional, you can best enhance your power, influence, and persuasiveness through which of the following strategies?**
A. Gain as much experience as you can in non-HR positions.
B. Present proposals for new HR initiatives to your CEO in terms of what needs to be done and how it will be done.
C. Build a reputation for never failing and for steering clear of unacceptable risks.
D. Focus your networking and relationship-building efforts on powerful individuals who are at least one rank above you in the corporate hierarchy.

Answer Key

1. C (chapter 2: The Necessity of Power)

2. B (chapter 3: Power Sources)

3. A (chapter 4: Influence)

4. D (chapter 5: Tactics of Influence)

5. A (chapter 6: Persuasion I)

6. D (chapter 7: Persuasion II)

7. B (chapter 8: The Knockout Presentation)

8. D (chapter 9: The Ethics of Power, Influence, and Persuasion)

9. B (chapter 10: Becoming an HR Star)

10. A (chapter 11: Enhancing and Leveraging Your Power, Influence, and Persuasion Skills)

Summing Up

In this chapter, you learned that:

- The HR profession has established credibility in some respects—namely, its body of knowledge and credentials—but it needs to do more to increase the esteem in which it is held.

- HR practitioners' personal credibility enables them to better exert their power, influence, and persuasion skills—further building their personal credibility and enhancing the profession's credibility overall.

- Techniques for building your personal credibility include creating a track record of success, acting with integrity, and networking.

- By using your personal credibility to exert your power, influence, and persuasion skills, you can overcome typical barriers to HR professionals' career advancement. Potent techniques include constantly learning and growing, developing trust-based relationships, and ensuring that your efforts always support your organization's goals.

Leveraging Chapter Insights: Critical Questions

- In your view, how do executives, employees, shareholders, vendors, and customers view the HR function at your company? Do these constituents hold HR in high esteem and respect the value it creates for your organization? Why or why not?

- What steps might you take to establish and sustain your personal credibility in your organization?

- How might you demonstrate your personal credibility in ways that enable you to exercise your formal authority as well as your powers of influence and persuasion?

- What obstacles, if any, have you encountered in moving forward in your HR career? What actions might you take to surmount those obstacles?

CHAPTER TWO

The Necessity of Power

You Can't Manage Without It

Key Topics Covered in This Chapter

- *Why power and power seekers are suspect*

- *The necessary role of power in organizations*

- *How dependencies restrain the concentration and autocratic use of power*

- *Three managerial approaches to power*

POWER IS A necessary feature of any system that involves people. In military organizations, every unit has one person vested with the power to command action. Even in collegial and democratic workplaces, someone must have the authority to say, "Thank you all for your input. Now, here is what must be done." Otherwise, none of the actions needed to move the company forward would be taken. Despite power's necessity, however, few people have a positive view of power. Indeed, many people distrust individuals who seek power. For HR practitioners, this tendency can be especially damaging if the organization has a culture that does not hold HR in high esteem as a profession.

This chapter discusses how people feel about power, why it is an essential aspect of organizational life, and how it is restrained by interpersonal dependencies. The chapter also evaluates three managerial approaches to using power.

Our Antipathy Toward Power

In many cultures, people view power with suspicion and fear because of its potential for coercion and corruption. We can all easily recall examples of power used for malignant purposes rather than for good: villains such as Adolf Hitler, Joseph Stalin, Pol Pot, and Saddam Hussein immediately come to mind. The use of power for malicious or self-serving ends is surely what moved Britain's Lord Acton to declare in 1887, "Power tends to corrupt, and absolute power corrupts absolutely." This sentiment is so well entrenched in the public consciousness that those who seek power often earn the suspicion and distrust of others. Indeed, many people feel that power should be withheld from those who most actively seek it. Because of this general antipathy toward power and power seekers, writes Rosabeth Moss Kanter, "People who have it deny it; people who want it do not want to appear to hunger for it; and people who engage in its machinations do so secretly."[1]

Given our antipathy toward power and those who hold it, it is no surprise that democratic political systems contain checks on power. These systems also specify measures to distribute power in ways that prevent it from becoming absolute or concentrated in too few hands. The founders of the American republic grappled with this issue. Their constitutional solution? Establish mechanisms that prevent the concentration of power in one branch of government and that protect the interests of minorities against the power of the majority. The U.S. Constitution's Bill of Rights checks power by specifying individual rights that government cannot abridge, no matter how powerful it is.

Power as Necessity

Paradoxically, neither society nor its organizations can function without the application of power. Government cannot fulfill its basic purpose without the power to tax and spend, to make laws, and to enforce those laws. Roadways would degenerate into chaos if police lacked the power to enforce traffic regulations. And our business enterprises would quickly go to pieces if boards and managers lacked the power to make and implement strategy, to hire and fire employees, and to compensate the workforce. Recognizing the necessity of power, democratic societies allow certain individuals and institutions to have power—as long as they use it within the bounds of policy, custom, or law, and in the service of ends that the majority accepts as legitimate.

As you saw in the introduction to this book, power is the potential to allocate resources and to make and enforce decisions. In an organizational context, this means that power gives someone the potential, among other things, to do the following:

- Determine compensation for employees

- Obtain funding, materials, or staff for key projects

- Gain access to important information

- Resolve disputes

- Clear away barriers to progress

- Determine key goals and marshal resources around them

These activities are critical to the business of management—whether in a company's HR department, marketing team, or some other component of the firm. Little would be accomplished if no one possessed the power to decide or act. The power to influence others is equally important. That power can be used to rally support for important goals and to motivate individual employees. All executives—HR and otherwise—need both types of power to succeed.

Paradoxically, society's intense distrust of individual power does not transfer fully to the workplace. In business, we expect that some people will have more power than others. In fact, many employees would rather work for managers who have organizational power ("clout") than for people who do not. A powerful supervisor can get them what they want: visibility, upward mobility, and resources. Working for a powerful boss also confers an aura of status on subordinates. In contrast, working for a powerless boss is like being left to stagnate in the outer darkness; subordinates of executives or managers who have little or no organizational clout feel powerless themselves and are usually dissatisfied with their situations.

Some evidence even suggests that powerless bosses are more likely to behave tyrannically toward their underlings. According to Kanter, "Powerlessness . . . tends to breed bossiness rather than true leadership. In large organizations, at least, it is powerlessness that often creates ineffective, desultory management and petty, dictatorial, rules-minded managerial styles."[2] This observation isn't all that surprising. Managers who lack real power cannot obtain the resources needed to fulfill their responsibilities. This leads to frustration, poor morale, and ineffectiveness among their subordinates—perhaps prompting the supervisor to crack down on them.

Thus, power used wisely in workplace settings is more likely to produce effectiveness and motivation than oppression and poor morale. Consider this hypothetical case of an HR information systems manager who, lacking organizational power, has become ineffective:

> *William enjoyed upward mobility during the first six years of his employment with Ultra Electronix. Hired as an HR information systems (HRIS) analyst, he made important contributions to the company's use of technology. Before long he was named director of HRIS. Thanks to his technical know-how and ability to work productively with managers from other units, William gained progressively more organizational power and influence—and a budget to match. Morale was high among his five direct reports.*
>
> *William's visibility and growing influence was abetted by his boss, Harold, the vice president of HR. Harold believed strongly in the value of technology and made sure that information on cutting-edge systems played a key role in technology decisions.*
>
> *William's standing in the company changed quickly, however, when Harold retired. Toni, Harold's successor, had come up through the traditional managerial ranks and put less stock in cutting-edge technology than William did. As far as she was concerned, benefits management, training initiatives, and incentive systems were the be-all and end-all of the HR function. So no one was surprised when the budget for information technology was cut 20 percent, forcing William to lay off one of his employees.*
>
> *Under Toni's regime, William felt his organizational power slipping away, and with it his ability to influence other managers and motivate his subordinates. He no longer had exciting projects to offer his people, nor did he have rewards to share. In his mind, work became routine and less meaningful. His direct reports no longer looked to him for mentoring or career development.*

TABLE 2-1

Symptoms and Sources of Powerlessness for Key Positions

Position	Symptoms	Sources
First-line supervisors	• Close, rules-minded supervision • Tendency to do things oneself, blocking of subordinates' development and information • Resistant, underproducing subordinates	• Routine, rules-minded jobs with little control over events • Limited lines of information • Few advancement prospects for oneself/ subordinates
Staff professionals	• Turf protection, information control • Retreat into professionalism • Resistance to change	• Routine tasks seen as peripheral to "real" tasks • Blocked careers • Easy replacement by outside experts
Top executives	• Focus on internal cost-cutting, producing short-term results, punishing failure • Dictatorial, top-down communication	• Uncontrollable lines of supply because of environ-mental changes • Limited or blocked lines of information from below

Source: Adapted from Rosabeth Moss Kanter, "Power Failure in Management Circuits," *Harvard Business Review,* July–August 1979. Used with permission.

Supervisors and managers need power to do their jobs. Lacking it, they exhibit the symptoms described in table 2-1. They develop into managers for whom no one with talent or ambition wants to work. Failing to possess and use power when the situation calls for it results in indecision, delays, and sometimes mischief. As Jeffrey Pfeffer aptly put it in his book *Managing with Power,* "[O]ne can be quite content, quite happy, quite fulfilled as an organizational hermit, but one's influence is limited and the potential to accomplish great things, which requires independent action, is almost extinguished."[3] People who will not touch the hot handle of power will not—and cannot—influence what happens around them.

Of Power and Dependency

Although power is essential for effective management, it doesn't necessarily come with the job. Newly minted supervisors and managers usually think that the formal authority attached to their positions will give them all the power they need to fulfill their responsibilities and carve out reputations for themselves in the organization. They believe that, like *Star Trek*'s Captain Picard, they need only describe what they want done and tell subordinates to "make it so." Then reality delivers a swift kick to the posterior. They find that they are not masters of the universe, but highly dependent on others: on their bosses, their subordinates, peers, suppliers, and other constituents.

Dependency is a fact of life in complex organizations, at every level, because of limited resources and the division of labor and information across many units. A person's acquisition of formal power does not eliminate his or her dependency on others. Consider these examples:

- Sarah, the founder of a busy HR consultancy, depends on each consultant that she has hired to handle his or her engagements effectively. Sarah is so busy generating new business and cultivating relationships with existing clients that her company would fall apart if any of the partners repeatedly mishandled engagements.

- William, the director of HRIS described earlier, depends heavily on the know-how of his professional staff to complete his unit's work. Those individuals must carry out their specific responsibilities without his having to micromanage them. William also depends on people who do not work for him— for example, the experts he hires to assess new technological advances. He needs their intimate knowledge of technology to determine which systems would best help his company and to make smart decisions about introducing new technologies.

- Judith is eager to advance her HR career. In this goal, she has come to depend on two individuals: her boss, who gives her

assignments that broaden her skills, and Linda, a senior executive with whom Judith has established a mentoring relationship.
Linda opens doors for Judith throughout the company and sees
that she is assigned to important cross-functional teams.

Each of these examples demonstrates how even people with formal authority depend on others for success. You'll learn more about
dependencies in the next chapter.

Using Power: Three Types of Managers

Assuming that people acquire the power they need to do their jobs,
how do they use it, and how does power motivate their behavior?
David McClelland and David Burnham studied these questions and
published their findings in 2004.[4] They found that a manager's approach to power is tightly connected to personal motivation and the
way he or she defines success. In effect, they described three types of
managers: affiliative managers, personal power managers, and institutional managers.

Affiliative Managers

In the view of McClelland and Burnham, the *affiliative manager* is
more interested in being liked than in having and using power to get
the job done. When such a manager is dealing with subordinates, his
or her decisions are heavily influenced by what will make subordinates happy and put them on the manager's side. Consequently, decisions are more ad hoc than consistent with the requirements of the
work at hand. Policies and procedures take a back seat to decisions
that make people happy with the boss. Of the three types of managers, this one is the weakest and least effective.

In their eagerness to be liked, affiliative managers fail to use
power for its intended purposes. The result is predictable: key goals
are not met. The case of General George B. McClellan underscores
this important point.

In the early part of the U.S. Civil War (1861–1865), General Mc-Clellan was entrusted with the Union's main army, to which he applied his exceptional talents for organizing and training. He built the Army of the Potomac into a powerful fighting machine and developed plans for seizing Richmond, the capital of the secessionist Confederacy. McClellan was popular with his soldiers and with many politicians, who affectionately called him "the Young Napoleon." McClellan basked in that popularity.

It seems that he was popular with almost everyone except his commander in chief, President Abraham Lincoln. Lincoln repeatedly urged McClellan to use his force to engage the enemy, but the general vacillated. He complained endlessly that he needed more men, more munitions, and more time to prepare. The few campaigns

Working for an Affiliative Manager

The affiliative manager is likely to jeopardize your career, for two reasons. First, this manager will not be consistent in making decisions and following policy. That means you cannot anticipate his or her behavior. Second, this manager is likely to lose status in the organization relative to people who know how to acquire power and use it effectively. Consequently, you'll be working for a weakened boss and may not get the resources and visibility you need to build your own career. Your best action is to look for a move—either within your organization or to another organization entirely if necessary.

If an immediate job change isn't possible, you'll need to take the initiative and make the best of the situation at hand. The following strategies can help:

• Diagnose the assumptions that have led to your boss's weaknesses. For example, is your boss averse to conflict? Concerned about not being liked? Fearful of taking personal responsibility? Convinced that others dislike being told what

continued

to do? Use observation and conversation to determine the problematic assumptions, then adjust your style to address your boss's concerns. For instance, if your boss doesn't assert his power because he feels uncomfortable with strong emotion, present a calm and reassuring demeanor at all times.

- Build connections with managers and executives from other departments. By cultivating positive, mutually beneficial relationships with these colleagues, you stand a better chance of gaining opportunities to showcase your competence. You also sweeten the odds of getting resources—an expert's opinion, a peer manager's advice, a few hours' assistance from another department's employee—that you need to accomplish your work.

- Go after important job assignments. Identify "stretch" assignments that would enable you to master the skills necessary to advance your career. Go after these assignments—openly expressing interest in them to your boss and speaking directly with the person in charge of allocating the assignments.

- Build your managerial skills and knowledge. No matter how familiar you are with the managerial role, you can always learn more. Seize advantage of managerial training programs, e-learning opportunities, books and articles on management, and other vehicles for further deepening your knowledge. The more you know about management, the better your ability to acquire needed resources and shape others' perceptions of your capabilities.

- Do good work. Exceed the performance standards your company has established for your role, constantly seeking ways to provide ever higher-quality work. Your achievements will help shine a light on your abilities, even if your boss won't provide the same visibility.

SOURCE: Michael Dobson and Deborah Singer Dobson, *Managing Up: 59 Ways to Build a Career-Advancing Relationship with Your Boss* (New York: AMACOM, 2000). Used with permission.

he did launch proved too timid or too late, or were terminated too quickly. Frustrated by his general's reluctance to use his considerable force, Lincoln sacked McClellan and turned the reins over to others. "My dear McClellan," Lincoln wrote in March 1862, "if you don't want to use the Army I should like to borrow it for a while."

McClellan enjoyed his status and his popularity with the troops and the public, but he didn't use the power he was given to pursue his primary responsibility. Do you know of managers like this—people who are reluctant to make tough decisions and apply their power? In many cases, the reason behind that reluctance is a fear of offending others or losing popularity. But these managers run the risk of getting a memo similar to the one written by Lincoln: "My dear Jones, if you are fearful of losing the friendship of your subordinates, you will be replaced by someone who has no such fear."

See "Working for an Affiliative Manager" for tips on handling the challenges of working for this type of manager.

Personal Power Managers

The *personal power manager,* per David McClelland and David Burnham, is a different creature from the affiliative manager. This manager's personal desire for power exceeds his or her need to be liked. Such an individual seeks power for himself or herself and for people on the team in order to get the job done. Unlike the authoritarian or coercive boss, who gains strength by making everyone around him or her weak, this boss generally manages in a democratic way. Subordinates like this kind of boss and often become very loyal. Their boss is not only strong; he or she makes *them* feel strong. On the negative side, these managers are power aggrandizers and turf builders, and not good institution builders. Consider this example:

> Steve, the vice president of corporate sales, is smart and aggressive, and a tough taskmaster. During his first year in his current post, he pushed out the three or four people who couldn't or wouldn't do their jobs, replacing them with individuals who had solid track records. "You people are on the best team in the business," he often tells his staff and sales representatives.

Steve is generous with his subordinates and stands behind them when they come into conflict with people in other departments. "We are sales," he likes to remind them during periodic pep talks. "Nothing happens in this company until one of us makes a sale. Nothing! That's something the other departments need to understand."

Although Steve has met the company's sales goals and has built high energy and morale in his unit, he has created friction with other departments—to the point that cross-functional collaboration has suffered. To Steve, every interaction with other departments is an opportunity either to defend his unit's prerogatives from encroachment or to expand its power at another department's expense.

Do you know any managers like Steve? If so, you've probably realized that they are not team players in the companywide sense. Fiercely competitive, they often take a combative stance in their interactions with fellow managers. And when they eventually exit the company for more powerful positions elsewhere, the subordinates they leave behind feel as though the air has been sucked out of them. Why? They gave their loyalty to an individual, not to the larger organization.

"Working for the Personal Power Manager" offers helpful guidelines for cultivating the most productive relationship possible with this type of supervisor.

Working for the Personal Power Manager

If you report to a personal power manager, expect to enjoy a high sense of team spirit within your unit. However, the boss may have so estranged other departments that you find collaboration with people outside your unit difficult. You may also find yourself forced to choose between the interests of your unit (i.e., your boss) and the interests of the company as a whole. In the long term, this may endanger your career with the company—especially if the personal power boss departs. Consider these suggestions for handling the situation:

- Be loyal to your boss—this type of boss demands and rewards loyalty—but only as long as loyalty doesn't require you to do anything that clearly goes against the interests of the company and its shareholders.

- Build and maintain your own broad network of contacts within the company; you'll increase your effectiveness and enhance your value to the organization instead of only to your boss.

- Develop a personal reputation for high integrity and standards; that reputation will help you if and when your boss leaves the company.

- Produce the highest-quality work possible. Your boss expects his or her team members to shine, and wants to praise you and your colleagues to managers of other departments.

- Develop an ability to tolerate the prickly moods that may arise in your boss if he or she gets into a conflict with another department. Avoid inadvertently escalating a bad mood by insisting on your boss's attention; rather, ask yourself what parts of your business can wait until later.

Institutional Managers

The most effective managers, say McClelland and Burnham, have something in common with personal power types such as Steve (see figure 2-1). They want power more than they want to be liked. But that's where the similarity ends. These *institutional managers* deploy power in the service of the organization, not in the service of personal goals. Generally, these people exhibit the following characteristics:[5]

- They are highly organization-minded.

- They have a strong work ethic.

- They are willing to sacrifice some self-interest for the welfare of the organization.

FIGURE 2-1

Assessing the Effectiveness of Manager Types

WHICH MANAGER IS MOST EFFECTIVE?

Subordinates of managers with different motive profiles report different levels of responsibility, organizational clarity, and team spirit.

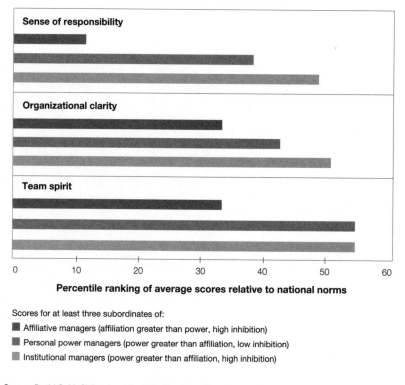

Percentile ranking of average scores relative to national norms

Scores for at least three subordinates of:

- Affiliative managers (affiliation greater than power, high inhibition)
- Personal power managers (power greater than affiliation, low inhibition)
- Institutional managers (power greater than affiliation, high inhibition)

Source: David C. McClelland and David H. Burnham, "Power Is the Great Motivator," *Harvard Business Review,* January 2003, 123. Used with permission.

- They believe in rewarding individuals who work hard toward organizational goals.

For subordinates who like to work hard and do a good job, these are the best managers to work for: they are mature—not egotistical and not defensive—and eager to reward performance. Consider this example:

Marion, the HR director for a large corporation, takes immense pride in her staff. She works hard to ensure that the department gets the resources it needs to provide top-quality services to the organization, and she takes pains to reward team members who excel at their jobs and understand how their daily work supports the organization's competitive strategy. For example, when Tim, a payroll administrator, recently offered ideas for cutting costs—one of the company's newly established strategic priorities—Marion praised his efforts to the rest of the department during a weekly status meeting. As a result of Marion's leadership style, her staff enjoys a high level of team spirit.

Marion also demonstrates a strong work ethic—tracking down the causes of errors made in her department, striving to provide ever-increasing levels of high-quality service, and putting in the hours needed to get the job done. When she asks her group to go above and beyond the call of duty in order to meet a difficult deadline, she works alongside her team until the job is done—then thanks everyone by taking them out to dinner.

Finally, Marion at times will sacrifice some self-interest for the good of her organization. For instance, she recently championed the promotion of one of her most valuable staff members to a higher-level position in another department. Though she regrets losing this employee and knows that it will be difficult to find someone to replace him, she also believes that an important part of any manager's job is to help his or her direct reports develop their professional skills and advance their careers. Supporting employees' career aims, Marion knows, helps her company retain valued workers and get the best performance from them.

See "Working for the Institutional Manager" for ideas on maximizing the value of reporting to this type of manager.

Figure 2-1 compares the effectiveness of the three management styles in terms of sense of responsibility, organizational clarity, and team spirit.

Working for the Institutional Manager

If you report to an institutional manager, congratulations: experts maintain that this type of manager is the most effective of the three discussed in this chapter. While working for an institutional manager, you can expect to see and hear substantial information about company goals and strategies. Your manager might even post updates on the company's financial performance in common areas.

Institutional managers tend to keep their eye on the organization's long-term aims at all times. They also go beyond the call of duty to support the company's strategic direction—working long hours, striving for constant improvement in performance, and using their power to benefit the company, not themselves or their department's narrow interests. To forge an even more productive bond with your institutional manager, consider applying these practices:

- Propose strategy-related ideas that come to mind during the course of your work. Your manager will appreciate your effort to support the company's goals.

- Demonstrate your own strong work ethic by pitching in as needed during crunch times and on strategically important projects—even if it means occasional substantial overtime.

- Take the initiative to learn as much as you can about your organization's strategic goals, competitive situation, and desired direction. The more informed you are about your firm's big picture, the more valuable ideas you can offer your boss.

- Frequently discuss with your manager how your daily work relates to the company's ability to achieve its high-level goals. Brainstorm ways to further strengthen the alignment between your efforts and the organization's strategy.

Altering Your Management Style

Can you change your management style? Yes, according to McClelland and Burnham. But you can do so only after you become aware of your current style. You can gain this awareness through careful self-assessment. For example, take stock of what you consider most important in your role: positive bonds with employees and peers, loyalty from your direct reports, ability to support the company's goals, and so forth. What do you strive for most? Your honest answers will shed light on your current style. Consider finding an executive coach who can help you assess your style. Objective feedback from peers inside and outside your company, as well as former employees who have moved on to other companies, can also be valuable.

Yet awareness of your management style has little value unless you follow up with behavior change. For example, if you find that you are an affiliative executive or manager and you want to become an institutional leader, you must adopt the behaviors of that type of person and make habits of those behaviors. Perhaps the most fruitful way to accomplish this is to identify and emulate a successful role model—someone who has the traits of an institutional leader. If you can, arrange things so that you report to that person or establish a mentoring relationship with him or her. If need be, observe the institutional executive or manager from a distance. Take note of how he or she makes decisions and works with peers, superiors, and subordinates. Then put into practice the skills and behaviors you observe.

Yes, power is necessary, and individuals embody and use it in various ways. You cannot manage without it. But if it is necessary, what are its sources? That's the subject of the next chapter.

Summing Up

In this chapter, you learned that:

- People generally distrust and fear power and those who seek it.

- Despite negative views of power, organizations cannot function without it. Most people prefer working for bosses who have and use power.

- New managers quickly discover that their power to act is limited by dependencies on others.

- According to two researchers, affiliative managers are ineffective users of power; they are more interested in being liked than in having and using power to accomplish goals.

- Personal power managers seek power and know how to use it. However, their use of power is often self-serving.

- Institutional managers, as described in this chapter, represent the ideal. They use power to advance the interests of their organization, giving those interests priority over their own.

Leveraging Chapter Insights: Critical Questions

- In your current role, what do you have power to do? What are the limits to your power?

- On whom are you most dependent to carry out your work? How do you manage that dependency so that you get what you need from those individuals?

- What type of leader—affiliative, personal power, or institutional—are you? Why?

- If you're an affiliative or personal power leader, what steps might you take to become more of an institutional leader? How might you mitigate some of the negative aspects of being an affiliative or personal power leader?

- What type of leader is your supervisor? If he or she is an affiliative or personal power leader, how might you manage the relationship?

CHAPTER THREE

Power Sources

How You Can Tap Them

Key Topics Covered in This Chapter

- *The power of position and its limitations*

- *How dependencies limit positional power*

- *Relationships with others as a source of power*

- *Using coalitions to increase relational power*

- *The law of reciprocity*

- *The sources of personal power*

- *An extended example of personal power*

- *Identifying power sources in your company*

POWER IS a necessary element of organizational work. But where does it come from? How do you and other executives and managers acquire it? Power in organizations generally has three sources:

- **Position.** Your position in the organization confers some level of formal power. For example, if you head the HR function and report to the CEO, CFO, or some other high-level individual, you likely have significant formal power.

- **Relationships.** Informal power stems from your relationships with others. For instance, if you build a coalition of managers to support a major initiative, you're exercising relational power.

- **Personal.** If you possess general knowledge, technical competence, and an ability to articulate ideas or a vision that others will follow, you generate power from within.

This chapter takes a close look at these three sources of power. Once you understand them, you'll find ways to increase your own power and use it to achieve your department's and company's goals.

Positional Power

Your formal position in the organization is one source of your power. That position is usually invested with a title, a set of responsibilities, some level of authority to make decisions and act, and control of specific resources. But neither a title nor a set of official responsibilities

lends *real* power. Instead, it's the authority to act and to control resources that others want or need that generates power. These resources include the following:

- Career-enhancing assignments for subordinates

- Permission to form a project and move it forward

- Approval of budgets, work plans, and vacation schedules

- The power to appraise performance

- Money (via control or influence over the budgeting process)

- Promotions and pay raises

- Materials and equipment

- Information

A key point to remember about positional power is that if you
use it merely to obstruct others from reaching their goals or to protect your turf, you'll fail in the long run. Others will recognize your
misuse of power and will find it difficult to trust you. You'll thus find
it increasingly harder to forge positive, mutually beneficial relationships in the workplace.

Formal positions in an organization carry with them a certain
degree of authority. The CEO, for example, is the ultimate arbiter of
decisions, barring vetoes by the board of directors. By virtue of his
or her position, the CEO can determine who is hired and fired, how
financial resources will be allocated, and so forth. This *power of position* is observable at many levels in an organization's reporting hierarchy. (See "HR's Power of Position.") An inventory manager will
usually have the final say on stock levels and reorder sizes. Although
her boss has the power to overrule her decisions in cases of serious
disagreement, what the inventory manager decides will usually stick.

Position confers authority to act within a certain scope but not
beyond it. The inventory manager, for example, may reign within her
defined domain but has no authority to act in others, such as marketing or finance. She can advise or share her judgment in those areas
but cannot command.

HR's Power of Position

Many HR professionals possess significant power of position: they occupy high levels in the organizational hierarchy. In one survey of HR professionals working in the United States, almost 25 percent of the respondents said that they reported directly to their company's CEO. Between 11.5 percent and 20 percent indicated that they reported to the HR director or the vice president of HR. Some wrote that they reported to the chief operating officer or the chief finance officer of their organization. In these positions, HR professionals have significant power to control essential resources and make important decisions.

SOURCE: Lisabeth Claus and Jessica Collison, "The Maturing Profession of Human Resources in the United States of America Survey Report," SHRM Global Forum, January 2004, 8. Used with permission.

Position also confers control over specific resources. For example, the safety manager for a commercial airline can keep a scheduled flight at the gate if conditions, in his opinion, warrant it. Even the CEO may be unable to overrule the safety manager's decisions.

It is tempting to rely on positional power and its inherent authority to motivate behavior and get work done: "I'm the boss, and this is what you must do." This is a particular temptation for newly minted supervisors and managers who have not yet identified or developed other sources of power. Those who lean heavily on the authority of their positions, however, may be surprised when that power fails to enlist the collaboration of subordinates. In many cases, subordinates resent being ordered around and respond with shoddy work or foot-dragging.

In an era when people are accustomed to challenging authority, pulling rank is seldom an effective use of power. Harvard professor John Kotter points to two reasons. First, managers depend on many people—including their own subordinates. Second, "virtually no one in modern organizations will passively accept and completely obey a constant stream of orders from someone just because he or she is the 'boss.'"[1]

Whether or not you use it, the power of position is highly visible to your subordinates. It is always in the "on" position and will always set you apart from your direct reports, who well know that you control their livelihoods. One manager interviewed for this book put it this way:

Subordinates see you as a member of a different caste, and as a person capable of helping or hurting them. This means that you must be careful in how you speak with subordinates. They listen carefully for clues to your moods and intentions, which are bound to affect them. Even remarks made in jest can have an unintended impact. For example, you may joke, "Well, if this project doesn't work, some people will have to walk the plank." That type of light-hearted remark reminds subordinates that you have the power to eliminate their jobs and incomes.

Another manager had this to say: "Like it or not, power differences between people determine their relationships. As a manager, you might want to maintain friendly relationships with subordinates. But forget about being friends. As long as you have the power to appraise their performance and to advance or retard their careers, you cannot be friends in the normal sense."

Here are a few tips for making the most of the power of position:

- **Invoke positional power only when absolutely necessary.** Recognize that few objectives can be accomplished through positional power alone. As an executive or manager, you depend on the help of other departments and your own subordinates to get jobs done. So use persuasion and other means whenever possible to get what you want.

- **Understand the boundaries of your positional power.** Don't try to apply it beyond those boundaries. For example, if you are the director of human resources, invoke your authority on all matters relating to your company's human capital but not on matters related to marketing or finance. In those areas, others have legitimate positional power.

- **Defend your positional power from encroachment by others.** Ambitious managers are always looking for ways to increase their power. Don't allow them to do so at your expense. For example, if your boss begins to meet separately with your direct reports to assign work or evaluate their performance, have a talk with him or her about lines of authority. Your boss's usurping of your authority and responsibilities will undermine your positional power and make it harder for you to do your job.

- **Help other executives and managers learn about and use positional power wisely.** Ensure that they understand the limitations of positional power and that they don't rely too heavily on it in their dealings with subordinates. In management training programs, make certain that teachers and facilitators discuss the nature, sources, and limitations of power.

Relational Power

Relational power is an informal power that emerges from your relationships with others. For example, a mentor has the power to influence the behavior of a protégé. A *coalition* is yet another example of relational power. Effective managers rely on coalitions when units must collaborate to get things done. Managers with very little positional power, for example, can wield substantial power if they form coalitions in support of their views. Let's consider each of these and other relational power sources and discuss ways to leverage them.

Building Power Through Coalitions

Coalitions enable weaker parties to gather the power needed to push through their proposals or to block those they find unacceptable. Collective action makes us strong. Coalitions are common in labor relations, politics, international diplomacy, and war. They are also eminently useful in business.

There are two types of coalitions you should understand: a *natural coalition* of allies who share a broad range of common interests, and a *single-issue coalition,* in which parties that differ on other issues unite to support or block a single issue (often for different reasons).

A natural coalition of allies usually endures, because its members share fundamental interests of substantial breadth. They see eye to eye on a range of issues. For example, a product development team and the head of corporate sales may share a common goal and act in concert when financial analysts attempt to block development of a new product line. These parties also have a common interest in projects that result in incremental improvement in existing products. Because of their broad basis of mutual interests, natural coalitions are difficult to break.

In contrast, a single-issue coalition of otherwise disassociated parties is generally less powerful for two reasons. First, their basis for collaboration is limited. Second, the coalition forms around a fleeting issue. Consequently, single-issue coalitions tend to break up faster than natural coalitions and are easier to defeat, especially if their opponents can divide and conquer. For example, a labor union and a nature conservation group might form a coalition to block an antiunion developer from building an office complex in a wooded area. Each party has its own reasons for joining the blocking coalition, and that difference makes it possible for the other side to put a wedge between them. If the property owner finds a different developer with a better track record in dealing with unions, the union is likely to withdraw its opposition to the complex, leaving the conservationists to fight alone. Or if the developer agrees to take steps to minimize the complex's environmental impact, the conservation group is likely to pull out, leaving the union as the sole opponent.

You can boost your relational power by joining coalitions of other executives and managers who have broad, common agendas. Take a moment right now to do the following:

- Ask yourself, "What workplace issues would I be more successful in managing if I were part of a like-minded coalition?"

- If a coalition is a feasible approach to exerting power on those issues, which individuals or departments would make logical and reliable allies?

If joining a coalition is a feasible approach, go for it. But don't be a passive participant. You will enhance your relational power in the company if you demonstrate leadership, trustworthiness, and a concern for the interests of your coalition partners.

Dependencies

Dependencies are a natural part of human society. In every dimension of our lives, we depend on other people for some things, and they depend on us for others. Indeed, complex organizations are bound up in mutual dependencies. For instance, market researchers need field data gathered by the company's sales representatives and funding provided by the marketing department. The marketing department, in turn, relies heavily on the quality of information provided by market researchers and by product inventories made available by the production department.

Here's another example—this one from HR. Suppose you're piloting a new performance management process that you believe will help align your company behind a major competitive strategy. To assess the initiative's value, you need unit leaders to start measuring their employees' and their own performance according to the new metrics and report the results. A permanent rollout of the program will depend on the quality of the results you get from the pilot. Thus you're also depending on managers and employees to deliver a high level of performance on the metrics you've established. Meanwhile, managers throughout the organization depend on HR to understand their business and needs, help develop performance measures that support the organization's strategic goals, help them find and hire employees who can support those goals, ensure that payroll and benefits are running smoothly, and provide other daily services.

Every part of a business enterprise can point to dozens of functional dependencies within departments and across departmental lines. None of these dependencies is a part of anyone's formal job description; you won't find them in any organization chart. Still, every one of them provides an element of relational power for someone.

What are *your* dependencies? Many new managers are surprised by how much they depend on others to get things done. But novice managers soon realize that dependencies constrain their options.

After all, none of us can easily command people who are in a position to withhold something we need. On the other hand, crafting positive relationships with others on whom you're dependent can boost your chances of receiving the cooperation and other resources you need from others.

So how much net power might you draw from dependency relationships? That hinges on two factors: (1) the dependence of other people on you (a positive factor) and (2) the extent to which you are dependent on others (a negative factor). Thus, you can increase your relational power by reducing your dependence on others or by making others more dependent on you—or both.

To better understand your dependency relationships, make a list similar to the one in table 3-1, which indicates the dependency relationships of Roland, an HR manager. Identify the people or departments on which you depend (and for what), and do the same for the

TABLE 3-1

Roland's Workplace Dependencies

I depend on ...	For ...
Lisa (clerical assistant)	Handling duplication of materials and arranging for audiovisual equipment and appropriate facilities for department-sponsored training programs
Carlos (finance)	Keeping me up-to-date on budget variances
Joan (information systems)	Generating quarterly and annual payroll reports
Tom (CEO)	Supporting HR initiatives aligned with the company's business strategy, and approving HR expenditures for these initiatives

... depends on me	For ...
Gwen (production manager)	Recruiting a pool of qualified applicants for open positions in her department
Karl (accounts payable)	Dealing with HR consultants to whom we owe money
Doris, Jean, Arnold, Max, Truman (my staff)	Obtaining the information, resources, and equipment they need to do their jobs, and providing timely, constructive feedback on projects for which they're responsible

people or departments that depend on you. This assessment will give you a capsule view of your dependencies and will suggest avenues for creating a more favorable situation—one that will boost your net power.

As you look for power-altering possibilities, consider the nature of your dependencies on others. How deep are they? Most will be benign, but others may constrain your freedom of action and thus weaken your ability to manage activities for which you have responsibility. A good example in table 3-1 may be Roland's dependence on Joan, the information systems (IS) manager, for timely payroll data. Information is a source of power in every modern organization, and an IS manager could hoard that power by keeping a tight grip on the gathering and dissemination of information. "Joan keeps our latest payroll data bottled up," Roland complains. "I have to beg for that data and rarely have it when I need it most."

Roland's dependence on Joan hurts his effectiveness as a manager. He should take steps to reduce or eliminate this dependence, perhaps by moving payroll data gathering and storage into the HR department, where he would have more immediate access. Another approach would be to take steps to make Joan more responsive to his needs—for example, perhaps by regularly checking in with her to see if she has been able to pull together the reports she needs. Doing so would increase his net power, all other things remaining the same.

After you've analyzed your dependencies on others, turn to the relationships in which others depend on you. Each of these relationships is a positive power factor from your perspective, and that power helps you be effective. For example, Karl, the accounts payable manager, depends to some extent on Roland for dealing with HR consultants to whom the company owes money. Karl will say periodically, "Roland, PeoplePro called to say that we're a few weeks overdue on their bill. Could you give your contact there a call to let them know we're on it?" Roland knows that his personal contact with vendors will help take a burden off Karl's shoulders. He also knows that Karl's dependence has from time to time given him some negotiating power with the finance department when vendors want special terms in their contracts. Deeper dependence by Karl might give Roland even greater negotiating power and a freer hand in negotiating more favorable contracts with vendors.

Take a minute to think about your dependency relationships. In particular, think about these two things:

- How you can increase your effectiveness and thus your value to others

- How you can increase others' dependencies on you

See "Handling Your Dependency on Your Boss" if you need guidelines on cultivating a positive, mutually supportive relationship with your supervisor. Whether or not you report to your company's CEO, you may also find "Leveraging Your Power Through a Strong CEO Relationship" helpful.

Handling Your Dependency on Your Boss

You can maintain a good relationship with your boss by being honest, keeping the boss informed, and being dependable in your work. Michael Dobson and Deborah Singer Dobson offer suggestions in their book *Managing Up*:

- Be supportive of what you and your boss are trying to achieve for the company, not competitive over resources or status.

- Give advance warning about problems, rather than trying to cover them up in the hopes that your boss won't notice them.

- Keep your word—providing information and other deliverables to your boss that you've promised, and following through on commitments you've made.

- Help your boss succeed by continually seeking ways to improve the quality of your department's work. You'll make your boss look good, as well as further strengthen his or her trust in your abilities.

SOURCE: Michael Dobson and Deborah Singer Dobson, *Managing Up: 59 Ways to Build a Career-Advancing Relationship with Your Boss* (New York: AMACOM, 2000). Used with permission.

Leveraging Your Power Through a Strong CEO Relationship

As an HR executive or manager, you are both a source and keeper of a critical resource: knowledge and information about your company's workforce. With the guidance and information you provide, your company can define and execute strategies to hire and retain talented employees with the right skills and competencies. You have the capability to formulate a strategy that will develop a workforce to meet your organization's goals.

For these reasons, you have a unique source of power. One way to leverage that power is to share workforce information with your CEO and offer ideas for using it for the company's good. These moves enable you to forge a strong relationship with your CEO, which in turns helps you gain the support and resources you need to implement your ideas.

Experts offer several guidelines for leveraging your power through a strong CEO relationship:

- **Align HR's goals with those of your organization.** Clarify your company's strategic objectives and identify HR goals that support those objectives. For example, if your company wants to be seen as on the cutting edge of innovation, you might identify HR goals such as cultivating a culture that encourages people to share ideas, think creatively, and take risks. Another HR goal that might align with the company strategy is to identify the skills and experience that employees in different parts of the organization must possess in order to support leading-edge innovation.

- **Familiarize yourself with HR technology.** By understanding and embracing new technologies—such as just-in-time online training—you can offer your CEO ideas for tapping such technologies' power. Savvy use of technology can help your company react more quickly to workplace changes.

Why? People will have easier access to the information they need to perform their work and strengthen vital skills.

- **Learn how to calculate return on HR investments.** Ask your CEO to fill you in on the company's business plan and key metrics it uses to assess performance. Then, when you're proposing a new HR program—such as a compensation plan or recruiting effort—explain how that program will ultimately affect key metrics and the company's business plan.

- **Support executives' job performance.** Your CEO needs executives and managers throughout the company to deliver top-notch performance on the job. You can help satisfy that need by providing the information and resources that those individuals require to deliver such performance. How? Understand what defines excellent performance in the executive and managerial ranks. Establish professional-development opportunities that will help these leaders excel. Ensure that your company has a solid succession plan in place, including strategies for identifying potential new leaders (including CEO candidates) and developing their talents. Provide your CEO with regular updates on retention rates, training efforts, and performance evaluations—which will help him or her spot top performers as well as those who can benefit from extra training or new assignments.

- **Move from presenting information to suggesting solutions.** During meetings and informal conversations with your CEO, don't limit yourself to presenting information. Also provide suggestions for *using* that information to solve your company's thorniest problems. For example, if you inform the CEO that your company's retention rates are worse than those of rival companies, offer ideas for improving retention.

SOURCE: Bill Leonard, "Straight Talk," *HR Magazine,* January 2002. Used with permission.

The Law of Reciprocity

Relational power can also be increased through a system of reciprocity. Whenever you provide professional services for someone else, a change takes place in the relationship. The other person feels compelled to offer you professional services in return. This is the *law of reciprocity*—an often tacit mandate by which we human beings expect every good deed to be repaid someday. Whoever invented our society must have been an accountant, because much of what goes on is based on the notion that "one good deed deserves another." We know instinctively that doing something for someone else creates an obligation for that person to return the good deed in some way sometime in the future. The original good deed is registered in the "accounts receivable" section of our personal balance sheet. A person who has many receivables has future money in the bank, so to speak, which provides some level of power.

For example, political bosses in U.S. eastern cities during the late nineteenth century got their poor and powerless constituents out of scrapes with landlords and the police. They helped them locate apartments and found places for them on the city payroll. On election day, the bosses called the debts in. They not only asked debtors to vote for them but also got them to campaign for them in their neighborhoods. In some cases, they even persuaded them to get other people to the polls and to cast more than one ballot. Reciprocity was the name of the game.

What does your balance sheet of professional services look like? Are you a net debtor or, like nineteenth-century political leaders, a substantial creditor? If you are a substantial creditor—if you have a large balance of "receivable" favors—take care that people don't exploit your generosity while having no intention of repaying it. Like a credit manager, you should determine which individuals have the capacity *and* the intention of reciprocating. How do you make that determination? Ask for a favor in return—then see what happens.

One of the interesting features of relational power is its independence from the formal power associated with your place in the organization. Thus, middle managers and staff personnel are capable of wielding power based on the many favors they have done for others (the law of reciprocity) and the extent to which more highly placed people depend on them. They may also find a source of power within coalitions.

Relationships serve as an important source of power, but you must be judicious in using them. Managers must sense when to tap these relationships and avoid overexploiting them.

Personal Power

The final source of power that bears mentioning is *personal power.* Personal power is what's left after the powers of position and relationships are stripped away. It is a function of the qualities and traits that others recognize in you. In most cases, these personal qualities include the following:

- Trustworthiness

- Relating well to others

- Expertise that others value highly

- An ability to communicate opinions and ideas in compelling ways

- Accomplishments that merit admiration and respect

- A charismatic style that engages others' emotions and allegiance

- Powerful and attractive ideas

- Enthusiasm and dedication to hard work

- An ability to enlist collaboration among colleagues

- Self-confidence

- Abundant physical energy and stamina

The sum of these personal qualities is a measure of someone's personal power. That power enables people to lead in the absence of formal authority and to influence the thinking and behavior of others over whom they have no organizational control. Consider the following example:

> Hard work and expertise in benefits management helped Philippa gain substantial recognition within BestCo, a large consumer-goods company. The idea of outsourcing some aspects of benefits management was new and radical when Philippa joined the company in 1985. But she had the know-how and foresight to recognize its potential. She also had the interpersonal skills to make a winning case for its adoption as BestCo's new benefits-management strategy, which she helped implement. That strategy proved highly successful, helping BestCo substantially lower costs and provide even better service to its workforce.
>
> After the new strategy was solidly rooted, Philippa began beating the drum for a related initiative: outsourcing management of multiple HR service vendors to one entity. "We can serve our employees even faster and better if we consolidate management of multiple vendors under one provider," she told anyone who would listen. "This will further free up the HR staff's time to invest in more strategic initiatives." Because of Philippa's reputation as an idea generator, people listened.

Do you have people like Philippa in your company? Are you one of these people yourself? If so, how are you and others like you regarded by the people above and below you in the hierarchy? People like Philippa generate considerable respect and attention based on the personal power they earn through hard work, forward thinking, regular contributions, and their ability to communicate ideas that interest others. They aren't always highly placed—indeed, they may not have much of a knack for managing—but their opinions are respected. These are the individuals to whom others turn for advice, information, and even direction. Consequently, they are often consulted when important matters are being discussed.

We need look no further than the late W. Edwards Deming, a leader of the quality movement of the 1970s and 1980s, to find an individual whose remarkable personal power made him an industrial legend. Deming embodied most of the personal qualities listed earlier. Although he practiced as a solo consultant and gained wide-spread notice in the United States only when he was well past normal retirement age, Deming's personal power changed the thinking and behavior of major corporations on four continents.

Deming (1900–1993) learned the principles of statistical process control (SPC) while working at AT&T during the 1930s with pioneering statistician Walter Shewhart. During World War II, Deming taught those principles to American manufacturing managers, helping them ensure quality, reduce waste, and save resources as they produced military equipment and munitions. After the war, Deming was invited by the Union of Japanese Scientists and Engineers (JUSE) to instruct its members in SPC principles.

Japanese managers and engineers viewed their American visitor as highly compelling. They viewed him as highly trustworthy because he told them to ignore "misguided" American manufacturing methods and to adopt others. They also respected Deming's expertise in the techniques of quality control and recognized that his ideas could transform and revitalize their war-torn industries.

By the early 1950s, quality had become the religion of Japanese industry, and Deming was its high priest. JUSE established the annual Deming Prize, which, even today, honors corporations that best adhere to Deming's principles.[2] By the late 1970s, Deming's ideas enjoyed a renaissance in his home country, making him one of the most sought-after lecturers and consultants to top management.

Deming exemplifies how an individual without organizational authority or material resources can influence others and shape the course of events. Chances are that you know of other people like him. What personal qualities account for their power? Do you share any of those qualities?

Personal Power and Informal Leadership

Chances are that you encounter many situations in which you must lead and manage when you are not the boss—that is, when you do not have formal authority over the people you need to work with and influence. This is commonplace in organizations that manage work through cross-functional teams. One or more team members may actually outrank the team leader. This is precisely the kind of situation in which personal power truly matters. To learn more about leading when you're not the boss, read appendix A, which offers a five-step approach to this challenge.

Rate Yourself

What is your personal power profile? Assessment tool 3-1 lists qualities generally associated with personal power. Rate yourself against each one. Then have one or two objective colleagues who know you well do the same. The combined ratings will give you a good idea of your strengths and weaknesses. If you eliminate those weaknesses, you will increase your personal power.

See table 3-2 for guidelines on leveraging and building your positional, relational, and personal power.

Assessment Tool 3-1
Your Personal Power Profile

Trustworthiness. Speaks the truth.

    Below Average   Average   Above Average

Ability to relate well with others. Understands the value of give and take.

    Below Average   Average   Above Average

Expertise that others value. Has knowledge or technical expertise that can translate into business success.

    Below Average   Average   Above Average

Communication skills. Can communicate views and ideas in compelling ways.

    Below Average   Average   Above Average

Accomplishments. Makes contributions that merit admiration and respect.

Below Average   Average   Above Average

Personal charisma. A style that engages the emotions and allegiance of others.

Below Average   Average   Above Average

Powerful and attractive ideas. Always thinking ahead of the pack.

Below Average   Average   Above Average

Focus and enthusiasm. Not easily diverted or discouraged.

Below Average   Average   Above Average

A welcome member of everyone's team. An ability to enlist collaboration among fellow employees.

Below Average   Average   Above Average

Self-confidence. Not shy about speaking up on important matters.

Below Average   Average   Above Average

Energy and endurance. Tireless in pursuit of key goals.

Below Average   Average   Above Average

Reliable. Always does what he says he will do. Can be counted on to have done his homework.

Below Average   Average   Above Average

Total in each category

____ Below Average   ____ Average   ____ Above Average

TABLE 3-2

Using and Strengthening Your Power Sources

Positional power	• Invoke it only when absolutely necessary.
	• Avoid trying to apply it beyond your position's boundaries.
	• Don't let others usurp your authority.
	• Acquire the skills and experience you need to advance to higher positions in your company's reporting structure.
Relational power	• Join coalitions of other executives and managers who have broad, common agendas.
	• Reduce or eliminate dependencies that weaken your ability to manage activities you're responsible for.
	• Deepen dependencies that enable you to manage activities you're responsible for.
	• Provide favors to people who can provide you with resources you need.
Personal power	• Deepen your understanding of personal power qualities: Think of an individual who possesses extensive personal power. Ask people who know this individual, "What is it about X that makes X a natural leader?"
	• Identify personal power qualities—such as trustworthiness, communication skills, and expertise—where you're weak.
	• Develop a plan for strengthening the qualities you've identified.

Where Is the Power in Your Organization?

To deal effectively with power, you must understand the power that you and others in your organization have. Like electricity, power is invisible, but you can feel and observe its effects. Start with yourself. What are your sources of power? Are they formal or informal? For example, does your title or position impart any special power? Who depends on you to get their work done? How many well-positioned peers, superiors, or subordinates owe you a debt? What resources do you control? Are you boosting your power through membership in a coalition? Do your personal qualities (communication skills, visibility, accomplishments, and so on) afford you special power? Is your power greater or less than that of others with whom you must deal?

Apply the same analysis to those with whom you interact—those above and below you in the chain of command, as well as people in other functions who are outside the chain of command. If you've been at your company for a long time, you can probably point to the people and the departments that have the most power. If you cannot, or if you're new to the company, look for power in these places:[3]

- **Departments or business units whose leaders have the highest salaries or that pay the highest salaries to newcomers.** Salary size is often a useful indicator of what top management and the board of directors value.

- **Departments or business units that have the most representation in top management and on the board of directors.** For example, some companies reflexively look to finance, the sales organization, or another function for their next CEO. Some companies are also looking to top HR executives to lead their organizations. For instance, Anne Szostak—who became CEO of Fleet Rhode Island in 2001—was formerly director of HR for the company. Thanks to her HR experience, she maintains that she has "a better appreciation of the pressures that the CEO faces . . . and this understanding helps me . . . in directing the goals of [our parent] company."[4]

- **The executive conference room.** When key decisions about strategy and resource allocation are made, who's at the table?

- **Physical proximity to the CEO's office.** The old notion of the palace court continues in our business organizations. People with power usually have offices in the headquarters building close to the top executive's piece of personal real estate.

You can make a rough measurement of your own power, or your boss's power, by simply checking these power indicators.

You now understand the three main sources of power in organizations: positional power, relational power, and personal power. Understanding these will put you in a much better position to tap the power you need to get things done on the job.

Summing Up

In this chapter, you learned that:

- The power or authority associated with formal position in the organization is observable at every level. It confers authority to act within a certain scope but is seldom sufficient to get things done.

- Relational power is informal power that emerges from your relationships with others. Some of these relationships represent dependencies, which can either enhance or limit your power.

- If you do a favor for someone else, a change takes place in your relationship with that person, who now owes you a favor in return. This is the law of reciprocity at work, which affects relational power.

- Coalitions represent a means to increase your relational power.

- Personal power is a function of one or many qualities: ideas, expertise, accomplishments, charisma, communication skill, and trustworthiness. These qualities impart power even when other forms of power are limited.

- You should understand where power resides in your organization. Salary size is often an indicator, as is proximity to the CEO's office and participation in high-level strategic discussions.

Leveraging Chapter Insights: Critical Questions

- How much power stems from your formal position in your organization? How can you make better use of that source of power?

- How much relational power do you possess? What steps might you take to strengthen this source of your power?

- In which coalitions, if any, are you a participant? Which coalitions might you join in order to further enhance your relational power?

- How much personal power do you wield? What personal qualities might you further develop so as to increase your personal power?

- Which individuals and departments in your organization have the most power? How do you know? What does this imply for how you can best accomplish your goals for the company?

CHAPTER FOUR

Influence

Your Mechanism for Using Power

Key Topics Covered in This Chapter

- *Influence as a mechanism for using power*

- *Why influence is a two-way street*

- *Enlarging your sphere of influence*

- *Using "currency" exchanges to build influence*

L IKE ELECTRICAL POWER, organizational power is only a potential. Real power is realized only through some form of expression. In organizations, power often expresses itself as influence: the ability to change, direct, or affect the behavior of others without ordering or threatening them. As an HR professional, you'll need to exert your influence with superiors, peer managers, and employees in order to serve your organization through accomplishing your department's goals.

Power created and held for its own sake has no value. Individuals may hope to use such power for self-protection or to serve their own ambitions, but in organizations, power has value only when people use it to accomplish legitimate goals. This chapter describes the limitations of direct power and explains how HR professionals can use their power indirectly to influence the outcomes they seek.

Power Versus Influence

As described earlier, power is the potential to mobilize resources and to influence others. In her book *Exercising Influence,* Kim Barnes makes the case that power is something you *have,* whereas influence is something you *do.*[1] For example, as a manager, you have the power to recommend that your staff members receive a pay raise, a promotion, or a termination letter. You can use that power to influence the direction and quality of your staff's day-to-day work. This supports the notion that power is purely a potential that must be tapped in some way to produce a desired outcome.

Influence is the mechanism through which people use power to change behavior or attitudes. Unlike power, influence can produce an effect without the apparent exertion of force, compulsion, or direct command. Of course, in some cases, people can and must express their power directly, as in the following situations:

- Controlling the allocation of resources

- Settling disputes

- Hiring, firing, and promoting individual employees

- Making task or project assignments

The direct application of power, however, has two important drawbacks. First—and perhaps most notable—the people on the receiving end of directly applied power may respond half-heartedly. The use of direct power circumvents the process of mutual agreement, involvement, and buy-in that normally produces employee commitment and good work in workplace situations. Unless they are already committed to a project or goal, people directed by power alone will do their work with simmering discontent. People who labor under the heel of direct power thus require close supervision. If the power in question lacks legitimacy, they may even rebel.

Second, applying power directly will eventually drain your power "battery." Executives or managers who rely repeatedly on direct power to get things done will eventually dissipate their supply of power, barring a recharging of the power battery. Leaders must therefore expend their direct power judiciously and only for the most important purposes. The application of power through influence demands less of one's power supply and is thus less likely to drain the battery dry.

Still, there are occasions when directly applied power is accepted, even welcomed. Perhaps the best example of these occasions is a crisis. During a crisis, the subtleties of consensus building, employee empowerment, and group decision making often get jettisoned because they take too much time or their outcomes are uncertain.

People caught in a crisis that threatens their well-being actually welcome a tough-minded, action-oriented commander who will take charge, make decisions, and direct their activities.

Democratic nations at war provide clear examples of how people respond positively to greater concentration of power at the top. Consider the experience of the United States, a country that prides itself on its separation of powers, its Bill of Rights, and its checks on governmental power over individuals. During the Civil War (1861–1865), World War II (1941–1945), and the current "war on terror," certain important powers shifted to the chief executive, and various individual protections were compromised in favor of the protection of society in general. Advocates of civil liberties objected and constitutional scholars were concerned, but the general public seemed comfortable overall with these changes. Most Americans seemed to want the government to have more power and to use it against foreign and internal enemies.

Even in times of crisis, however, effective leaders understand that they can enhance their success by applying power indirectly—that is, through influence. Here are a few examples of influence through indirectly applied power:

- Framing the issues of an important debate

- Encouraging people to identify with organizational goals

- Enlisting collaboration between cross-functional units

- Encouraging high standards

You can apply any of the sources of power cited earlier—positional power, relational power, or personal power—to these forms of influence. In each case, however, your intended outcome is the same: to encourage other people to do what you want them to do, but *willingly and enthusiastically*. This may make you recall the well-known episode in Mark Twain's *Tom Sawyer* in which Tom convinces some other boys that painting his Aunt Polly's fence is fun and is an honor. He is so compelling that they insist on taking over the chore for themselves—and even pay Tom for the privilege.

Let's consider the first of the examples of influence cited earlier to illustrate how you might apply power indirectly through influence.

Influence Is a Two-Way Street

When you think about influence, envision it as a two-way street. To influence effectively, you must open yourself to influence by others. People who influence without subjecting themselves to influence in the process are simply applying direct power.

Executives and managers who open themselves to influence by their peers and subordinates gain more respect and acquire more influence—and successes—than those who resist others' influence. Openness to influence from others, even from subordinates, has two important consequences. First, it visibly demonstrates that you trust and respect others. And to gain trust and respect, you must first extend it to others. Second, openness enables you to acquire valuable information and insights about your company and the environment in which it operates. People who resist influence close themselves off from signals about the business environment—putting themselves at risk of being blindsided by unfolding events.

Consider the story of how senior executives at General Motors in the early 1980s failed to let their own quality and reliability (Q&R) managers influence them. Those managers tried to convince their bosses through empirical data that Japanese automakers were rapidly outpacing GM on quality issues that mattered to customers. Their case fell on deaf ears—at least for another two years. The top people clearly could influence their Q&R people, but they seemed immune to influence from Q&R.[2]

How can you begin opening yourself to influence from others? Start with active listening. Through active listening, you capture what the other person has to say while signaling that you are alert and eager to hear it. Here are some active-listening tips:

- Keep your eyes on the speaker.

- Take notes as appropriate.

- Resist the urge to formulate your response as the other person is talking. Give the speaker and his or her argument your full attention.

- Pay attention to the speaker's body language. Gestures, posture, and facial expressions are often just as revealing of the other person's feelings (if not more so) as are words.

- Ask questions to get more information and to encourage the speaker to continue. Questions also indicate that you are paying attention and interested in what the other person has to say.

- Periodically repeat in your own words what you've heard to ensure that you understand and to let the speaker know that you've processed his or her message: "So, you're saying that . . ."

You can also demonstrate openness to influence by using open-ended questions during conversations with other people. Open-ended questions are those that cannot be answered with a simple yes or no. For example, avoid saying, "That's an interesting idea. Do you think it will solve our problems?" This question invites a yes or no answer, neither of which will provide valuable information. Instead, say something like, "That's an interesting idea. How will it solve our problem?" Or, "That's an interesting idea. What have others said about it?" These open-ended questions invite the other person to express his or her idea more fully and provide you with more information.

But being open to influence requires more than lending an ear to others' opinions and ideas. You must also translate those opinions and ideas—the good ones—into action. If you listen to others and then merely do exactly what you originally intended to do, they'll conclude—rightly—that you haven't taken them and their ideas seriously. Result? They will likely decide that you are not open to influence. People respect and have confidence in leaders and managers who take their ideas seriously. That respect and confidence in turn make them open to influence by these same leaders and managers. However, people quickly lose respect and confidence in those who ask for their ideas but never take them to heart.

Your Sphere of Influence

Most of us are familiar with the concept of a *sphere of influence:* the domain in which one can effectively exert influence. In geopolitics, a nation's sphere of influence is a physical area within which the nation has a high level of—if not dominant—political influence. Thus, Latin America and the Caribbean have traditionally resided within the United States' sphere of influence. Southeast Asia and North Korea fall within China's sphere of influence. The influence of these two powers is strongest among their closest neighbors and among those with whom each nation has ideological, language, and commercial ties. The United States and China also exert strong influence over countries that depend on them for military, political, or financial support. The two powers' influence is weaker among countries that are either physically distant or lacking in those ties. We generally conceptualize spheres of influence as a set of concentric circles in which influence is strongest near the center and weaker as the distance from the center increases.

In business organizations, people behave similarly. For example, a manager intent on expanding her influence may promote or hire "her people" for key posts and give them substantial resources. Their loyalty to her ensures the manager of a high level of influence.

As in geopolitics, your personal influence is likely to be strong in some spheres and weak in others. The strength of personal influence derives from two elements described in an earlier chapter: one or another form of power (positional, relational, or personal) and the depth of others' dependencies on you. Consider the following two examples:

Caroline is the director of the HR department for her company. She has positional power by virtue of her title. In addition, she has built a reputation for getting results from HR programs and for generating good ideas. This personal power has given her leverage with the finance department, which controls corporate resources. Whenever her department needs more money in its budget, the CFO will give Caroline a hearing—if not the money—because of the returns she has produced from other funding.

Daniel is a corporate space manager. His job is to provide office space and furnishings for each department in his company. Outside his own small staff, he has no formal, command authority. Nevertheless, Daniel exerts broad influence in the company. The managers of every department depend on him to provide the floor space they need to do their work, and they go out of their way to maintain good relations with him.

Both Caroline and Daniel have spheres of influence that extend beyond the boundaries of their formal authority. Caroline's influence stems from her exemplary performance; Daniel's, from his control of an important resource on which others depend. To document insights about your own degree of influence, see assessment tool 4-1.

Obviously, your ability to influence people and events hinges tightly on your sphere of influence. So if you want to be more influential, you must find ways to expand or strengthen your sphere. You can do that in the following ways:

- Increasing your power—either positional, relational, or personal

- Finding ways to project your power into areas that are strategically important to you

- Creating deeper or broader dependencies by others

- Opening yourself to influence by others

Be strategic in your efforts to extend your influence, giving priority to the people who have the most potential to help you carry out your objectives. For example, for an HR manager, it is surely more critical to your success to build your influence with the heads of major departments than to extend your influence to others. So as you diagnose your sphere of influence, answer this question: *where is my influence most needed?* After you've answered that question, you must find a way to create that influence. The next chapter can help.

Assessment Tool 4-1
Map Your Sphere of Influence

1. Take a moment to map out your own sphere of influence. At the center of a piece of paper, draw a circle, and write "Me" in the circle. Around this circle, write the names of people over whom you exert influence. Include their position in the company. Arrange these names around your circle such that those over whom you exert the strongest influence are closest to your circle, whereas others range farther away. The people over whom you exert the least influence should be farthest away from your circle. Be sure you consider your company's board of directors, CEO, senior executives, non-HR managers, and employees within and outside the HR department. Also take into account external individuals—such as vendors, customers, media, and so forth.

2. Look at the map of your sphere of influence. Where is your influence strongest? Consider people over whom you have formal authority, as well as other individuals. With people over whom you have little or no formal authority, what explains your influence over them?

3. In what important arenas is your influence weak? What explains these weak areas?

Increasing Influence Through Currencies of Exchange

In their popular 1989 book *Influence Without Authority*, scholars Allan Cohen and David Bradford introduced the concept of *currencies of exchange* to help business people understand how they can acquire and expand their organizational influence. In these authors' view, currencies are the coinage of influence. They are the resources—goods and services—that a manager can offer to a potential ally in exchange for that person's cooperation. "Because they represent resources that can be exchanged," Cohen and Bradford write, "currencies are the basis for acquiring influence. If you have no currencies in your treasury, you do not have anything to exchange for what you want."[3]

Think for a moment about the currencies you have at your disposal—the goods and services you can use to build influence with your superiors, peers, and subordinates. By using your currencies ethically and appropriately, you benefit your organization; your peers, supervisors, and direct reports; and yourself. For example, for a subordinate, giving that person a challenging new assignment or public recognition of his or her achievements might be a highly valued currency. For a peer, goods in the form of the free use of some empty offices in your department might be much-appreciated currency. For your boss, you might offer your help in conducting research and analysis that she needs for an upcoming presentation to the board of directors. No matter what tangible good or intangible service you provide to someone else, the fact that the person values it means that you have some influence with him or her.

What is the key to using currencies effectively and appropriately? Discern what other people want and value. You gain that understanding when you move beyond a superficial level of knowing what motivates, inspires, and concerns people. What really matters to them? What are they trying to accomplish in their careers? What threatens them or stands in the way of their success? How does their view of the world and the organization differ from yours? If you answer these deeper questions, you will position yourself to make exchanges and influence the people with whom you do business.

See assessment tool 4-2 to assess your currencies.

Assessment Tool 4-2
A Checklist of HR Currencies

Review the following list. Put a check mark next to each form of currency that is available for you to use in building your influence. (Space is provided for additional forms of currency that might come to mind.) Then develop a plan for using those currencies to exert influence.

- ☐ Reassurance and emotional support that can help someone through a difficult time

- ☐ Public recognition of someone's achievements

- ☐ Empty offices that someone might value using

- ☐ Computers and other equipment or supplies that someone might need

- ☐ A staff member who could provide a few hours of assistance to another manager who is temporarily short staffed

- ☐ Assistance on a project that someone else is struggling with

- ☐ An introduction to an influential individual who someone wants to meet

- ☐ Access to powerful individuals whose attention and support someone might need

- ☐ The ability to make someone feel good about himself or herself—for example, through simple compliments, expressions of appreciation, or a request for their opinion or advice

- ☐ The ability to mediate a conflict between two other people in ways that benefit both parties

continued

☐ A genuinely positive performance review

☐ An opportunity for someone else to communicate his or her ideas—for example, through an article published in the company newsletter

☐ The ability to protect someone from unreasonable demands or criticisms coming from someone else

☐ The power to put in a good word for someone who wants an influential person's attention and consideration

☐ _____

☐ _____

☐ _____

Summing Up

In this chapter, you learned that:

- Influence is a mechanism through which people use power to change behavior or attitudes. Unlike power, influence can produce an effect without the apparent exertion of force, compulsion, or direct command.

- To have influence *on* others, you must open yourself to influence *from* them.

- Active listening and the use of open-ended questions can help you demonstrate openness to influence.

- The strength of your personal influence derives from two elements: one or another form of power (positional, relational, or personal) and the depth and breadth of others' dependencies on you.

- You can use the currencies (goods and services) at your disposal to build influence with others in your organization. These currencies may take such forms as technical assistance, information, the lending of space or equipment, a plum assignment, and so on.

- The key to using currencies is to understand what others want or value and provide currencies that satisfy those needs.

Leveraging Chapter Insights: Critical Questions

- With which individuals in your sphere of influence is your influence weakest? What steps might you take to strengthen your influence on these individuals?

- Take inventory of the currencies of exchange you have at your disposal. What are they?

- Think of the people with whom you must increase your influence in order to better carry out your responsibilities. What forms of currency would they value most? If you don't know, what steps can you take to find out? Which of your currencies of exchange might each of these individuals value most? What currencies of exchange would you want in return?

CHAPTER FIVE

Tactics of Influence

Six Mechanisms You Can Use

Key Topics Covered in This Chapter

- *Framing an issue to influence the outcome*

- *Using information to influence thinking and outcomes*

- *Understanding how growing complexity gives technical experts greater influence*

- *Leveraging your organization's hierarchy*

- *Using invisible social networks*

- *Exerting influence by helping to assimilate new leaders*

N OW THAT YOU'VE learned the general concepts of influence, it's time to think about tactics for translating your power into influence. Only by exerting influence can you win support for HR programs and initiatives and ensure that your ideas are implemented in your organization. This chapter examines six mechanisms for projecting influence: framing, information, technical authority, organizational hierarchy, invisible social networks, and assimilation of new leaders.

Frame the Issue Your Way

A *frame* is a mental window through which we view reality or a particular problem. For example, twenty years ago, concerns about the existence of nuclear weapons were framed in terms of a possible missile exchange between the world's two superpowers: the United States and the Soviet Union. Such an exchange could be triggered by an insane person working in a missile silo or by an erroneous radar report that the other side had already launched its rockets. Some people worried that one side or the other would make a preemptive strike. Today, however, people frame the issue of nuclear weapons in markedly different terms: they now worry about the prospects of rogue nations or shadowy terrorist groups getting their hands on these lethal weapons.

Unless we make a concerted effort to do otherwise, we frame reality in terms of our key concerns, interests, closely held beliefs, and prejudices. Thus, a dermatologist who meets someone for the first time is likely to observe a patch of sun-damaged skin on that person's forehead—something the rest of us wouldn't notice. When we walk into a gathering of economically successful people, we are likely to see opportunities to make new acquaintances and learn something new about personal success. A real estate salesperson walking into the same gathering will likely see a roomful of potential home buyers and sellers. The well-worn expression "If you're a hammer, everything looks like a nail" is a humorous way to describe the power of framing.

Framing an issue or agenda for others is a powerful way to exert influence. As Jeffrey Pfeffer has written in *Managing with Power*, "Establishing the framework within which issues will be viewed and decided is often tantamount to determining the result."[1] Consider this example:

> *The executive team at Benson & Haynes had convened to discuss a proposal presented by David Shelton, manager of HR. Shelton had suggested that the company develop online, self-paced training courses to prepare newly hired salespeople for their responsibilities. The company had never used e-learning resources before, and the team members had questions about the proposed courses' potential benefits and costs.*
>
> *Meg Galloway, the senior financial person at the table, quizzed Shelton about the projected increase in sales that the courses might generate, and the costs of developing and implementing the courses. She was far from enthusiastic. "Based on your projections, this program would have a positive net present value, but just barely," Galloway said. "And the rate of return is below what we demand of new projects."*
>
> *Nate Burke, the marketing executive, picked up where Galloway left off, asking for more details about costs and Shelton's method for generating his sales-increase projections. Shelton could see that the meeting was going to be a predictable evaluation of his proposed project, using sales and costs as the frame of reference. Unless he acted quickly, the value of e-learning for this company, and its potential impact on the company's future growth, would never enter the discussion.*

To everyone's surprise, Shelton didn't respond to the numbers issues. He politely deflected the first round of questions and launched into something unanticipated. "This proposal isn't about the financial impact of a single project," he began. "It's about an opportunity to break out of the rut we've been in for the past ten years by putting ourselves on the leading edge of technology and education. It's about an opportunity to help our sales force obtain the just-in-time learning they need to familiarize themselves with our products and match the right offerings with the right customers."

The assembled executives became more attentive. Shelton had hit two hot buttons: educational innovation and customer satisfaction. They began asking different kinds of questions that focused not on sales and costs but on recent advances in online instruction and the connections between e-learning and companies' ability to serve customers.

In this example, Shelton decisively reframed the discussion—a useful tactic for exerting influence. What gave him the power to do this? It wasn't formal, positional power, because he was outranked by the executives in the room. Perhaps it was Shelton's personal power—his record of accomplishment, his recognized expertise, or the power of his ideas—that allowed him to reframe the discussion.

Take a moment to think about workplace issues that are important to you. Are others viewing them through the right framework? If not, how can you use your influence to reframe those issues? Can you apply your positional power or relational power to make it happen? What elements of personal power can you draw on to reframe people's thinking? Also think about how you can influence others to identify with organizational goals, to collaborate, and to adopt high standards.

If you get people to look at issues in a different way, you will have influenced them through framing.

Increase Your Influence Through Information

It is often possible to influence people and the direction of debate through the presentation of compelling and irrefutable facts and numbers. Consider the following scenario:[2]

Sandra Van Drew, HR director for Arco Corporation, a large consumer-goods company, is meeting with fellow executives to explore strategies for controlling health-care costs. She has an idea that she knows will generate intense resistance, but she believes the idea is a good one. Her proposal? Pay hospitals bonuses for taking steps to improve the quality of care they provide—such as computerizing doctors' orders to prevent errors. Sure enough, when she floats the idea during the meeting, her colleagues immediately bristle. "I thought we were trying to reduce costs," says Tom Gormley, the CFO. "And how exactly can we prove that quality of care has gone up?" asks Pat Hogan, the CEO.

"I realize this looks costly in the short run," Van Drew says. "But I know it will reduce costs in the long run." Hogan asks her whether she's prepared to prove her point. Van Drew responds: "The National Committee for Quality Assurance, which as you know evaluates managed-care organizations, has created a tool that calculates company cost savings in terms of decreased sick days and increased productivity when health-care quality improves. By reducing the number of days our employees are out sick by 25 percent, I calculate that we can save $500,000 a year."

Hogan and Gormley seem pleased with these numbers, but they're still concerned about how to measure quality of care in order to determine bonus payments to hospitals. "From what I understand," says Gormley, "not all quality-measurement tools are created equal."

"That's true," Van Drew answers. "For example, most accreditation is voluntary, so health plans and other providers don't have to participate in the reviews. For that reason, we have to understand how ratings organizations gather data and measure quality." She lays out a broad selection of possible quality metrics based on both patient ratings (such as doctors' communication skills) and clinical performance (including whether patients are able to carry out normal daily activities after receiving care).

Reassured by the depth of Van Drew's research and intrigued by the potential cost savings that the hospital-bonus idea might generate, Hogan and Gormley agree to consider her proposal. "If you could look further into the metrics question," Hogan says, "we'll meet again in two weeks to discuss possible ways to peg bonuses to quality-improvement activities."

This scenario demonstrates how information can influence people and the course of events. In business, that influential information usually takes the form of financial figures. Naturally, the validity of those figures is critical. In their widely read book *Relevance Lost: The Rise and Fall of Management Accounting,* Thomas Johnson and Robert Kaplan explain how sloppy cost accounting gives false signals, encouraging managers to support unprofitable products and projects even as they shut down their true sources of value creation.[3] In other cases, advocates use information selectively, just as an attorney will present all the facts that support his or her client while keeping silent about those that do the opposite. Thus, an individual who develops a reputation for solid objectivity, rationality, and truthfulness—hallmarks of personal power—can use information to influence internal debate and key decisions. Sandra demonstrated these qualities by explaining the source of the calculation tool she used and by acknowledging that her colleagues were right about the difficulty in measuring health-care quality.

So take a moment to consider the important HR debates raging in your organization. These may be about allocation of raises among competent and exceptional performers, emphasis on promotion from within versus hiring new blood and expertise from the outside, or the best ways to manage skyrocketing health-care costs. Whatever the case, think about the information that could influence those debates. If you can provide accurate, relevant, and objective information on the key issues facing your company, you can influence the debate—and increase your own personal power.

Enhance Your Influence Through Technical Authority

Many important decisions involve technical information over which generalist CEOs and executives have no mastery. Consequently, they look to people with this mastery for guidance, creating opportunities for influence. Consider this example:

Fred and Cynthia were co-owners of a small but growing information technology (IT) services company. Between the two of them, they knew almost everything about setting up IT systems, Web site development, and data storage for the dozens of small client businesses they served. They were prototypical techno-geeks.

Unfortunately, their knowledge did not extend to the many other areas of expertise required by successful, growing businesses. They were clueless about employee benefits, taxes, sources of expansion financing, and other matters. Sensing their own weaknesses, Fred and Cynthia hired George, a young but experienced manager with an MBA degree. He was no digital wizard, but he was knowledgeable in matters of business strategy and operations. Within six months of joining the company, George had made a major mark on the business. He convinced the owners of the merits of abandoning their partnership in favor of a corporate form of business. Working with local bankers, he negotiated a refinancing of the company's debt at better terms and established a line of credit. He also put his HR hat on and set up a retirement plan for the two owners and participating employees. And he helped Fred and Cynthia understand the importance of developing a five-year strategy for their business.

As time went by, Fred and Cynthia came to rely more heavily on George's business acumen and advice. George's influence grew even stronger as he gathered additional knowledge about information technology.

You've undoubtedly experienced situations like this one in your own work, where one individual's technical expertise has given him or her exceptional influence. Today, technical specialists exert substantial influence in business and government. For example, company executives who reached the top through marketing or finance can appreciate the benefits of having a knockout e-commerce site, but they are usually unfamiliar with the details of creating and operating one. What differentiates a powerful site from a weak one? What does it take to build one? Who needs to be part of the building process? What will it cost? Lacking answers, they inevitably turn to technical experts, who, in the end, have substantial influence over the decisions and monetary outlays made at the top by nontechnical executives.

Do you have technical expertise on which company decision makers depend? If you do, think about the many ways you can employ your expertise to influence important decisions. If you lack technical expertise, consider acquiring some through on-the-job or formal training.

Maneuver Within Your Organization's Hierarchy

In the business arena, hardly anyone has a good word to say about organizational hierarchies—those reporting structures in which powerful bosses at the top drive decision making down to less and less powerful workers at the bottom. Yet the widespread aversion to hierarchies only testifies to their durability. Despite their unsavory reputation, corporate hierarchies remain the basic structure of most, if not all, large organizations.

Why do hierarchies persist? According to some experts, hierarchies deliver real practical and psychological value, and they fulfill our deep need for order and security. They also remain the most workable and effective structures we human beings have invented for performing large, complex tasks.

Hierarchies are by nature authoritarian. They comprise multiple ranks, layers of executives and managers, and sharply defined differences in power, control, and rewards. Take a stroll through any organization, and you'll likely hear people using language such as "climbing the corporate ladder," "pulling rank," and "corporate big-wigs." But by understanding how to maneuver within your company's hierarchy, you can still project your influence.

Despite the rigidity of most organizational hierarchies, there's plenty of room for you to exert influence. As we've seen, formal authority is only one source of power, and it goes only so far. Direct reports may meet most of their manager's demands—if those demands are presented respectfully. But for the rest, that manager needs to exercise his or her influence skills. And as you well know, formal authority is of little use to managers in their dealings with peers.

So that leaves informal influence as the best method for navigating within your organization's power hierarchy. According to Stanford professor emeritus Harold Leavitt, the best way to extend your influence within a hierarchy is to strengthen and exercise the following interdependent skills: pathfinding, problem solving, and implementing.[4]

Pathfinding

Based on your knowledge of your company's vision and desired direction, define a vision for your own department and your work. Ask, "What direction does HR need to take in order to help the company achieve its objectives? What do I want to accomplish, and what ideas do I want to propose, to help make HR's and my company's vision real?" For example, do you see a future in which HR is radically improving the company's use of contingent workers? Vastly improving the quality of benefits administration through partnerships with high-performing service providers? Overhauling the company's executive-development programs so that the organization boasts superior bench strength and a rock-solid succession plan? What pictures of your possible future get you most excited?

By defining a compelling vision and having a clear sense of direction for yourself and your unit, you can more easily see what actions need to be taken and what problems need to be solved. You therefore sharpen your own and others' focus.

Not surprisingly, pathfinding requires an understanding of your company's desired direction and your unit's and your own capabilities. It also means bucking the all-too-common notion that only the "top dogs" in an organization generate a vision for everyone else to follow. Though your company will almost certainly have a high-level vision, you must develop one for yourself and your function as well. Otherwise, you'll have nothing to guide your daily actions.

Problem Solving

Armed with your vision, you can identify needed actions and solutions to problems that must be handled in order to realize your vision. For example, if you've envisioned a radical new strategy for using contingent workers, what steps must you take to determine the optimal mix of temporary workers, consultants, and part-timers?

How will you solve the problems of selecting the right staffing agencies and calculating the return (in terms of cost savings or productivity increases) on contingent-worker initiatives?

Problem solving requires intellectual abilities: you gather information, make difficult decisions, calculate probabilities, and devise and implement optimal solutions—activities that courses in finance, statistics, economics, and accounting can help you master. Although many solutions are implemented through formal hierarchical controls (such as the budgeting process or task assignments), you need to balance your use of hierarchy with some "politicking" to gain support for your proposed solutions. Coming up with a great-looking solution is one thing; putting it into action, quite another. Why? During the implementation phase, you'll need the commitment and support of other people to carry out your solution. The adage "people support what they helped to create" is true.

So, while you're gathering information and mulling over possible solutions to a problem, be sure to consult the people around you. Ask them what *they* think of your idea, and whether they have additional suggestions or concerns. Invite them to provide additional information, statistics, and data that can further inform your decision. At the very least, you'll send the message that you respect and value others' views—something that goes a long way toward winning support.

Implementing

To put your ideas, solutions, and decisions into action, you have to implement them—which requires the support and cooperation not only of your direct reports but also of others in the corporate hierarchy over whom you have little or no authority. For instance, to execute a new contingent-worker strategy, you'll need peer managers throughout the organization to give you information about their staffing needs and budgets—something they may resist doing if they feel they're too busy or they don't agree that using more contingent workers is a good idea.

Effective implementers rely on their emotional savvy to influence and motivate others to help carry out their ideas. In terms of day-to-day activities, emotional savvy manifests itself as building trust by modeling behavior you'd like others to demonstrate. (For instance, by providing information that peer managers need from you, you boost your chances of getting the information *you* need from them.) Emotional savvy also means listening to, supporting, and encouraging others—even if, rationally speaking, all of this seems like a waste of time. By exercising your emotional savvy, you get people to *want* to do the things you need.

How can you master emotional skills? Reading books and attending workshops can help. Also consider observing individuals whom you view as effective at motivating others. How do they communicate with people above, below, and around them? How do they behave? What personal qualities do they possess? Practice demonstrating such behaviors yourself if you need to strengthen this skill.

To operate effectively within an organizational hierarchy, you need at least a modicum of all three skills—pathfinding, problem solving, and implementing. You can also seek ways to forge cross-organizational connections with others in the company, to balance the vertical power structure that characterizes corporate hierarchies. Strategies for creating horizontal connections include forming or joining alliances and coalitions, seeking out common ground and shared interests between different parts of the company, and assembling cross-functional task forces or project teams that encourage participants from every corner of the organization to share ideas and solve problems together.

Leverage Invisible Social Networks

In every organization, there are webs of relationships through which people exchange information, collaborate, and engage in informal contact during the workday. These *social networks* are invisible: they don't show up on formal organizational charts. Indeed, they often differ substantially from the formal reporting relationships shown on the organizational chart.

For example, as an HR professional, you may have frequent hallway conversations or drop-in visits from people who pass your area on their way to the lavatory or copy machine. These impromptu exchanges constitute social-network activity, because you're bound to discuss ideas and learn about one another's expertise, challenges, and concerns while chatting. Other individuals may frequently come to you specifically for information. For example, the CFO drops in to ask if she can see those cost analyses of that vendor management software platform you've introduced recently. Or the head of marketing suggests meeting for lunch to talk about ways to better manage the contingent workers who will be working in his department over the coming months.

Likewise, you reach out to others for needed information, expertise, or collaboration, or take advantage of physical proximity or specific gatherings to interact with others. For instance, perhaps you swing by the IT director's office to ask her how things are going with the new HR module that has been added to the company's enterprise resource planning system. Maybe you spot the CEO's administrative assistant lunching in the cafeteria; you end up joining him and learning that the CEO was intrigued by a new HR policy you proposed recently and has some questions about it.

Social networks span organizational boundaries and comprise individuals who reside at all different levels within the corporate hierarchy. Like most human phenomena, they can be double-edged swords. On the one hand, they're difficult to proactively manage precisely because they're invisible. Thus, problems can crop up in a social network that can hurt the organization. For example, one individual in a network may become a bottleneck because so many people rely on him or her for information.

At the same time, social networks also offer enormous advantages. Through such networks, people can develop communities of best practices, generate innovative ideas, and carry out major change initiatives. For instance, a key information source in a network might help convey important messages about a large-scale initiative to others throughout the company.

Who makes up social networks? Experts have identified several types of network members:

- "Central connectors" participate in a disproportionate number of direct relations in the network. This can make them valuable sources—or turn them into bottlenecks if they become over-burdened by requests for information.

- "Boundary spanners" connect their own department with other departments or networks in the company.

- "Information brokers" communicate across subgroups in a network, preventing the network from fragmenting.

- "Peripheral people" have few or no connections in a network. They need space to operate on the fringes or, in some cases, require help to get better connected so the network can benefit from their expertise.

The healthiest, most valuable social networks are marked by variety and balance. For example, they contain all the member types just listed. Moreover, the people in them have known one another for varying lengths of time, possess a broad range of expertise, and connect with individuals above, on par with, and below them in the company's reporting hierarchy. This variety and balance yields important benefits. To illustrate, your connections with people above you in the reporting hierarchy can enable you to acquire resources. Connections with peers can lead to valuable brainstorming. And connections with people below you in the hierarchy can yield valuable technical information and expertise. Variety in the length of time you've known various members of your social network can ensure that you're not hearing the same old ideas over and over again—or hearing too many new and untried ideas all the time. To gauge the quality of *your* social network, try your hand at completing assessment tool 5-1.

By taking an active role in enhancing and fine-tuning your social network, you can greatly extend your influence throughout

Assessment Tool 5-1
How Healthy Is Your Social Network?

For each of the following statements, circle "yes" or "no." The more "yes's" you have, the healthier your social network.

1. I exchange information and collaborate with people above me, on the same level as me, and below me in the corporate reporting hierarchy.

   Yes   No

2. I exchange information and collaborate with people in other parts of the organization besides my own.

   Yes   No

3. I exchange information and collaborate with people in other physical locations besides my own—other floors in the building, field sites, other offices that the company occupies, and so forth.

   Yes   No

4. I leave time open in my schedule to invite serendipitous interactions with people in my social network.

   Yes   No

5. I invest enough time in maintaining social-network relationships that are important to me.

   Yes   No

6. I've known some people in my social network for a long time; others, for a medium length of time; still others, for a short time.

   Yes   No

7. The people in my social network embody a broad range of expertise.

Yes   No

8. No one in my social network seems overburdened by his or her participation in the network, nor does any member seem too isolated in the periphery.

Yes   No

SOURCE: Rob Cross and Andrew Parker, *The Hidden Power of Social Networks* (Boston, MA: Harvard Business School Press, 2004), chapter 5. Used with permisson.

the organization and help the network generate even more value for the company. Consider these techniques:[5]

- **Meet regularly with your network members.** Brown-bag lunches, off-site gatherings, virtual meetings, and other get-togethers help members explicitly acknowledge the existence of their network and identify ways to address problems (such as information bottlenecks) and extract the most value from the network. These gatherings also help members and newcomers get to know one another—a vital ingredient for strengthening the network's connectivity.

- **Help network members sharpen their awareness of one another's expertise, background, and interests.** A network's connectivity improves when members know something about one another's professional *and* personal backgrounds, skills, and interests. Online or hardcopy cards listing network members' current roles, contact information, areas of expertise, professional background, and personal quirks can help introduce people to one another. Time and again, businesspeople say that learning something personal about a new colleague—even if on a minor level—can greatly strengthen the sense of connectedness. These cards, for instance, might contain entries such as "Person you'd most like to have lunch with," "Ideal vacation you've never taken," "Hidden talents," and "First job or weirdest experience."

- **Cultivate trust among network members.** Social networks generate more value when members trust one another to have their best interests at heart. But in many companies, people from different departments lack trust—usually owing to an "us versus them" mentality. To help build trust throughout your social network, model trustworthiness yourself, as well as encouraging it in others. For example, when someone asks that certain information remain confidential, honor that request. Ensure that your words and deeds match—don't tell someone one thing and then do another. Communicate face-to-face as frequently as possible, to signal your interest in network members. Send the message that you trust others—for example, by providing someone with access to a limited resource without expecting something in return.

- **Correct unproductive network behaviors.** If you notice yourself or other network members increasingly turning to the same small number of individuals within the network for specific expertise, take steps to avoid "network lock-in." Create ways for network members to inform one another of new expertise they've developed since the last time they interacted. Watch carefully for political tensions, too—which often arise from personality differences or contrasting approaches to business and work. A professional coach can help two people talk through their differences.

- **Help other managers use social networks to "onboard" new employees.**[6] The more quickly new employees become embedded in their social networks, the faster they can make a contribution. Educate managers throughout your firm on how to leverage social networks for faster onboarding. For example, encourage managers to hand out first assignments that require newcomers to build relationships with a wide variety of people to get their work done. Managers can also assign newcomers to cross-functional project teams that expose them to a broad network of resources. Upon completion of an assignment, managers should ask not only "What have you accomplished?" but also "Whom have you talked to?"

For additional guidance in assessing and getting the most from your social network, see appendix C.

Pave the Way for New Leaders

As an HR professional, you're uniquely positioned to help new leaders at all levels assimilate into your organization.[7] Successful assimilation means ensuring that a new leader quickly grasps the company's major challenges and goals; forges connections with others above, on par with, and below him or her throughout the organization; and communicates his or her vision for the company or unit in question. Moreover, leaders recruited from inside the organization have just as much need for help with assimilation as do leaders coming from outside. That's because a newly promoted leader will face a whole new set of responsibilities and challenges that may bear little resemblance to his or her previous role. That person will also need to cultivate a new set of relationships based on changing responsibilities and challenges. (See "Assimilating a New CEO" for guidelines on handling the unique challenges that arise when a new chief executive is joining your company.)

In your role, you have unusual opportunities to enhance your influence with new and upcoming leaders, thus extending your influence throughout your organization. Why? By helping leaders assimilate, you demonstrate your knowledge, expertise, and awareness of the company's high-level needs. You thus earn new leaders' trust, respect, and appreciation—all qualities that increase your influence.

In many companies, the responsibility for designing and implementing an assimilation strategy resides in the HR department. For this reason, it's important that you either serve as or designate an "HR touchstone" who will partner with new leaders through the assimilation process. The HR touchstone needs to strike a delicate

Assimilating a New CEO

In handling the assimilation of a new CEO, you have the best possible opportunity to extend your influence. After all, if you can demonstrate your ability to help the new chief executive hit the ground running, your reputation for being a talented advocate as well as supporting the company's goals will likely spread throughout the organization.

Consider these tips for assimilating a new CEO:

- **Play a role during the executive search.** Help the board of directors establish criteria for selection before they fall in love with particular candidates. Ask, "Given where our organization is in its life cycle, what ideal characteristics do we need in the new CEO?"

- **Get to know the new CEO before he or she arrives.** Learn whatever you can about the new chief executive before his or her first day on the job. Talk with people from his or her preceding organization, as well as with individuals who know the new leader by reputation. Read articles about the new leader in the business press.

- **Initiate contact.** Before the new CEO starts, contact him or her and offer to meet outside the office, in a relaxed, social setting, to get acquainted and share information about your company's workforce and key human resource strategies and programs. Come with specific information about where the company stands regarding its workforce, and what changes need to be made. Rather than using "HR-speak" and minutiae, focus on key metrics such as the match between the workforce's skills and the organization's goals, key problem areas, important strengths, retention and turnover ratios, average sales per employee, cost of goods per employee, and costs of benefits. Ask what the CEO needs to know on an ongoing basis. Explain what you've done so far to address any problems. Describe who the peak performers are in the company, and what concerns employees have overall. Explain your ideas for making the company an employer of choice. Show that you understand the company's big picture, not just the HR part of the business.

- **Assess the new CEO's style.** In your early meetings with the new CEO, try to assess his or her style. How does he lead? How does she prefer to communicate? What does he envision in terms of moving forward with strategic planning?

- **Show that you can assist with the difficult decisions.** If your new CEO was hired to turn around an ailing company, housecleaning may soon follow. Take the lead, helping the CEO identify nonperformers and establishing a process for purging mediocre people.

- **Get the CEO's message out to the workforce.** Communicate his or her vision to your staff, explaining changes they need to make and ways in which they meet the new boss's approval. Also help the CEO get the message out about who he or she is and how things will change with the new leadership. Build a CEO visibility and communications plan, setting benchmarks at thirty, sixty, and ninety days. Brainstorm symbolic initiatives that the CEO might take to reinforce his or her message and demonstrate that this is a person who can make things happen. For example, when New York mayor Rudy Guiliani set out to eradicate graffiti on city buses and trains, the initiative didn't necessary help him accomplish his sweeping goal of reducing crime in the city, but it did send the message that he meant business and could get things done.

SOURCE: Robert J. Grossman, "Forging a Partnership," *HR Magazine,* April 2003. Used with permission.

balance: advocating for the new leader with whom he or she is part-nering, while also ensuring that the organization's objectives are met.

Assimilation is a process that unfolds over time. You can help fuel the process through a combination of facilitating, coaching, raising awareness, and intervening where necessary. As you think about the best ways to assimilate new leaders in your organization, consider the distinctive goals characterizing each stage of the process:

1. **Anticipating and planning.** Your assimilation strategy should include activities such as understanding the stakeholder relationships that will be most important to the new leader, preparing those stakeholders for the leader's arrival, identifying the competencies of the leader's surrounding team, preparing his or her team for arrival, and gaining the outgoing leader's support for the newcomer.

2. **Entering and exploring.** During this stage, you need to help the new leader set priorities; score small, early wins; make a good first impression on the rest of the company; assess organizational culture; and build relationships with his or her supervisor, peers, and direct reports.

3. **Building.** In this phase of assimilation, you explain past change attempts that took place in the organization, coach the new leader on handling resistance to new change efforts, create cross-organizational network-building and boundary-spanning opportunities for the leader, and help him or her make difficult staffing decisions.

4. **Contributing.** Here you need to help the new leader modify his or her strategies and approach as needed, based on feedback from the workplace. With your help, the new leader should also be able to further extend his or her network of influence, identify issues in the company that require large-scale change, and broaden his or her leadership scope by empowering others.

This discussion of influence is far from exhaustive. However, it suggests some of the principal tactics that HR professionals can use to influence others. The best lessons, however, can be found in your own organization. So be alert. Watch how the most respected and effective people in your company influence you and others. Use the most effective and ethical of these influencers as your teachers.

Summing Up

In this chapter, you learned that:

- A frame is a mental window through which we view reality or a particular problem. You can influence people's thinking and their decisions by establishing the frame.

- Information is another lever of influence. Just be sure that it is compelling and irrefutable.

- You can use technical authority to increase your influence. Because of the complexity of modern business and everyday life, many people—including key decision makers—have come to rely heavily on the advice and input of technical experts.

- Your organization's hierarchy offers opportunities for you to exert influence.

- By understanding and proactively leveraging the invisible social networks in your company, you can extend your own influence as well as help these networks generate important benefits for the organization.

- Assimilating new senior leaders is an avenue for influence that HR professionals are especially well positioned to use.

Leveraging Chapter Insights: Critical Questions

- Think of issues you're currently embroiled in at work. How might you frame those issues in ways that encourage others to support your ideas?

- Think of the key individuals in your organization with whom you wish to have more influence. What information do you possess that may help you increase your influence with each person? How might you augment your inventory of information?

- What technical authority do you possess in your role? How might you use it to exert more influence throughout your organization?

- Where in your organization's power hierarchy might you find opportunities to exert your influence? What structures might you establish to encourage horizontal and vertical collaborations that are not reflected in the organizational chart?

- How would you gauge the health of your company's invisible social networks? What steps might you take to make those networks even more beneficial for your company?

- How would you gauge the effectiveness of your strategy for assimilating new leaders? What actions might help you strengthen that strategy?

CHAPTER SIX

Persuasion I

The Basics

Key Topics Covered in This Chapter

- *The necessity of persuasion in management*
- *The four elements of persuasion*
- *Influence mapping as a guide to knowing who to persuade*
- *Various types of audiences and decision styles*
- *Characteristics of a rock-solid case*

A FEW MONTHS AGO, Margaret was promoted to manager of benefits administration. Last week she read an interesting article about a new benefits program that many other companies like hers are implementing. The program involves setting up a vacation donation policy, by which employees give vacation and other paid time off to others for a specific cause—such as serious illness or crisis.

Margaret believes that implementing this program will yield important benefits for her company. For example, it will likely enhance morale and employee loyalty, increase productivity, and reduce absenteeism and turnover. She'd like to convince her boss and other key players in the company of the program's value.

Though she is certain that the organization would be better off instituting the vacation-donation policy, she recognizes the obstacles ahead of her. For one thing, determining which employees are eligible for the program and how donated vacation time should be valued will be difficult and may require input from the company's legal counsel. Margaret knows that some of the individuals who will evaluate her proposal—such as the head of the legal department and the chief finance officer—will likely resist her idea because of such concerns. She has some influence over company decision makers, but they all outrank her. What should she do?

Margaret must employ persuasion to achieve her goal. This chapter explains why persuasion is important and introduces its basic elements.[1] But before we begin, try to answer each of the following questions.[2] They will help you assess your current persuasive abilities.

- Do you know how to make your arguments interesting to others?

- When you attempt to persuade someone, do you effectively adapt your manner of speaking to the type of person you are speaking to?

- Do you have a sense of how high to set your goals when trying to change someone's thoughts or actions?

- Can you sense the best time to attempt to change someone's mind on an issue of importance to you?

- Do you support your ideas with reasons that others find compelling?

For managers at all levels in an organization, persuasion is the primary means of changing others' behavior and affecting decisions. In this sense, effective persuasion is a form of power and a tool of influence. To persuade is to use argument or entreaty to get others to adopt a belief or demonstrate a particular behavior. Talented persuaders have the power to capture an audience, sway its opinions, and convince opponents to align with their cause.

What exactly is persuasion? *Persuasion* is a process that enables a person or group to change or reinforce others' attitudes, opinions, or behaviors. It can take place in a single meeting or over time through a series of discussions. Persuasion is a skill that's essential for success in all relationships—personal and business alike. What's more, persuasion is not only a matter of making a rational case but also about presenting information and ideas in ways that appeal to fundamental human emotions. It's about positioning an idea, approach, or solution in a way that appeals to others.

Persuasion blends art and science. It's an art in that it requires the ability to establish trust. It's a science in that it is based on the disciplined collection and analysis of information, a solid understanding of human behavior, and well-developed communications skills. By mastering this mix of art and science, anyone can enhance his or her persuasive skills.

Why Persuasion Is Important

Persuasive skills have virtually infinite applications. An HR director advocating a new benefits program, an employee lobbying for a pay raise, a sales manager pitching the benefits of a new product line to a customer, a purchasing manager convincing a supplier to expedite shipment of an order—these are only a few examples of persuasion situations. We draw on our persuasive skills every day, usually without realizing it.

Changes in the business world have made persuasion a more critical managerial skill than ever. Here are two reasons:

- The days of executive command-and-control have given way to a world increasingly characterized by cross-functional teams of peers, joint ventures, and intercompany partnerships. Command-and-control is often seen as either illegitimate or counterproductive in this new world.

- Many people in the workforce have grown up questioning authority. They do not respond well to being told what to do; they respond best when persuaded of the logic and benefits of doing particular things in particular ways.

Clearly, formal authority no longer gets executives and managers as far as it used to. To do their job—accomplishing work through others—leaders must persuade others rather than simply issue orders.

The Elements of Persuasion

Persuasion requires preparation and planning. This fact is something we rarely think about, even though most of us engage in persuasive activity on a daily basis. Persuasion also involves these four elements:

1. Credibility

2. An understanding of your audience

3. A solid argument

4. Effective communication

We treat the first three of these elements in this chapter and the final one in chapter 7.

Building Credibility

Credibility is a cornerstone of persuasion. Without it, your audience will dismiss your proposal. Consider the time-honored fable of the boy who cried "wolf" too often. This child sounded the alarm among his rural neighbors whenever he thought that a dangerous wolf was on the prowl. After much commotion, these warnings were found to be baseless, and the boy lost his credibility. When a wolf did appear, no one listened to him.

Your own credibility manifests itself in two ways:

- **Your ideas.** For you to strike others as credible, your ideas must be perceived as sound. For example, the new human resource information system you have proposed must make sense in light of current market conditions, technology, and business concerns. Also, you must have thought through all ramifications of your proposal.

- **You as a person.** Other people must view you as believable, trustworthy, and sincere. Generally, these are personal qualities you must earn over time through working with others. Have you demonstrated these personal qualities?

We can think of credibility in terms of this simple but powerful formula:

Credibility = Trust + Expertise

The more trust you earn and the more expertise you accumulate, the more credible you *and* your ideas become.

Trust

When people trust you, they are inclined to see you as believable, well informed, and sincere. They know that you will respect their interests and will not act in ways that undermine those interests. They also view you as possessing a strong emotional character (a steady temperament) and integrity (honesty and reliability). Those qualities reinforce your appeal, and, in turn, make people more inclined to accept your ideas. In contrast, if people view you as untrustworthy or unreliable, they will discount or disregard everything you say.

Here are several ways to earn people's trust:

- **Tell both sides of the story as you understand it.** If you are proposing something, be candid with people about the pros and cons. For example, in proposing a new benefits program, give an objective estimate of the best, worst, and most likely outcomes regarding the program's costs, effectiveness, and other aspects.

- **Deliver on your promises.** Do you always come through on promises and commitments you've made? If you do, people will feel confident that when you say you'll do something, you'll do it.

- **Keep confidences.** If someone shares information in confidence, respect that confidence unless you are legally or ethically obliged to do otherwise. For example, suppose a newly hired department head says, "I'd like your opinion on how to establish a more positive working relationship with Janice, the head of finance. Our relationship seems to have gotten off on the wrong foot, and I'd like to improve it. I think I could really benefit from your expertise in this sort of situation. But I don't want Janice to know that I've talked with a third party about this." If you agree to this confidentiality, then stand by your promise. By demonstrating respect for confidential information, you develop a reputation for trustworthiness.

- **Be consistent in your values.** Almost everyone can point to friendships and successful working relationships with people with whom they disagree on important issues. Consider the example of the late U.S. president Ronald Reagan, a Republican and staunch political conservative, and the late Speaker of the U.S. House of Representatives, "Tip" O'Neill, a liberal Democrat. The two men were miles apart in their views on the role of government. Nevertheless, they managed to develop a trusting working relationship. How? Each respected the other's consistent adherence to his core values. Each could count on the other to behave in ways that were true to those values.

- **Encourage the exploration of ideas.** Listen to others' concerns in order to encourage dialogue and demonstrate your openness to their perspectives. Establish an environment in which people can share their ideas and know that their opinions are valued. This is much different from an environment in which people are chided and ignored if their views are out of step with those of the boss.

- **Put the organization's best interests first.** People will trust you and your ideas more if you can demonstrate that you have the broader organizational interest in mind. For example, suppose you help a valued subordinate get promoted to a different department. You hate to lose a top-notch team member, but you accept the idea that helping others develop their professional skills is part of your job as a manager and that the subordinate will perform with excellence in the new position. In helping your subordinate, you earn the trust not only of that one person but also of peers and other subordinates, who tell themselves, "She puts the company's interests ahead of her own."

Trust between people doesn't arise overnight. It develops over time and through a series of many personal interactions and observed behaviors. By *behaving* repeatedly in a trustworthy manner, you earn a reputation for *being* trustworthy.

Expertise

Like trust, expertise helps you build credibility. People perceive you as having expertise when you exercise sound judgment and demonstrate a history of successes. To build or strengthen your expertise, follow these guidelines:

- **Research your ideas.** Find out everything you can about the idea you're proposing—by talking with knowledgeable individuals, reading relevant sources, and so forth. Collect data and information that both support *and* contradict your idea. These moves will help you familiarize yourself with the strengths and weaknesses of your position.

- **Get firsthand experience.** Nothing is as powerful as demonstrated expertise. For example, if you plan to advocate a new method of HR technology, get out of the office and talk with people who understand and use the technology and can describe its complexities. If possible, try your hand at using the technology, so you can see for yourself how it seems to work. This experience will help you understand nuances you could never learn from books or secondhand sources.

- **Cite trusted sources.** Back your position with knowledge gained from respected business or trade periodicals, books, independent reports, lectures, and acknowledged experts—both inside and outside your organization. It's always smart to demonstrate that you are not the only voice supporting a particular point of view.

- **Prove it.** Launch a small pilot project to demonstrate that your ideas will work. For example, if you're advocating development of a new interview process, conduct a limited experiment with the process to generate firsthand information about its benefits. If your pilots uncover weaknesses, develop practical remedies for them.

- **Master the language of your topic.** Workers in most fields develop their own language, including buzzwords. This is true in the fields of HR, finance, information systems, investment management, materials management, and countless other endeavors. You need to master the language of your field if you want to persuade people who work in these fields. So pay close attention to language during meetings, industry conferences, and other business gatherings. Make sure that you understand the true meaning of that language—and use it appropriately in persuasion communications.

- **Don't hide your credentials.** If appropriate, let people know about any experience you have or relevant advanced degrees you've earned. For example, an HR generalist who has just earned his SPHR (Senior Professional in Human Resources) certification may want to ensure that his CEO knows of this accomplishment, in the hope that the CEO will consider him for a more senior HR management position or give him more strategy-related HR responsibilities. But note that in some companies, publicizing academic credentials is considered bad form. Doing so might hurt your credibility if your colleagues firmly believe that it's a person's ideas that count, not his or her degrees.

- **Team up with credible allies.** Enlist the help of people with established credentials to augment your own expertise. These allies might be other managers or executives with specialized training or experience, an outside consultant, or even a customer. Their standing in the field will bolster your own.

- **Gather endorsements.** People are often swayed by testimonials from respected, authoritative sources. If other departments or companies are currently enjoying success with the practices or products you advocate, then gather and publicize their remarks. For instance, suppose you've received approval to conduct a pilot employee-referral program. In this case, you might gather testimonials from employees and managers who have participated in or have been hired through the pilot. Using their testimonials, you could publicize the success of the pilot and thereby boost your chances of receiving approval to roll out a formal version of the program.

By establishing your trustworthiness *and* expertise, you build the credibility you need to get your audience's attention and agreement. But to take the next step in the process, you also need to understand your audience—including knowing how they make decisions.

Understanding Your Audience

No matter how credible people find you and your ideas, you still must understand your audience. Specifically, you need to do the following:

- **Identify decision makers, key stakeholders, and the network of influence within your audience.** Which of these people are supportive of, in opposition to, or neutral regarding your argument? What are their interests, and how do they view their alternatives?

- **Analyze your audience's likely receptivity.** Given what you've sensed so far about your listeners, what are the chances of the overall audience's embracing your idea?

- **Determine how your audience will make the decisions you hope to influence.** Will they decide through consensus? Majority rules? Some other method? Who do you need to convince of the value of your idea in order to control the decision-making process?

Identify Centers of Influence

In some persuasion situations, you'll present your proposal to one person; in others, you will make a presentation to several people, perhaps individually or in a single group session. In either case, you must understand that the opinions of some people hold more sway than those of others. In most cases, your true audience will usually consist of a subset of the people to whom you're presenting your idea. This subset may comprise a mix of the following:

- Decision makers

- Key stakeholders

- Influencers

Decision makers are the individuals who can approve or reject your idea. Many persuasion situations involve several decision makers. For example, if you want to hire an additional employee for your unit and you're lobbying your boss for the funds, she may not be the only person you need to persuade. Perhaps your boss's supervisor has the final say. Ultimately, your persuasion efforts must address the concerns of decision makers, even if indirectly.

Stakeholders are the individuals directly affected by the acceptance of your proposal. For example, unit managers in your company are stakeholders in performance-management policies. If you define a new policy that requires managers to collect additional forms of data on employees' performance, these managers' daily responsibilities will change significantly. They may feel that they're too busy to supply the information required by the policy. Not surprisingly, they may strongly resist it.

To identify key stakeholders, think of all the individuals who will be most affected by acceptance of your proposal. In most cases, these will include not only the person to whom you're presenting your proposal but also peers, direct reports, customers, superiors, and board members.

Influencers are individuals who participate indirectly in the decision-making process. They provide advice and information to key stakeholders and decision makers. For example, suppose you're the company's recruitment manager, and you want to persuade the IT department manager to redesign the company's Web site to include an updated careers and recruitment area that supports your department's employment branding efforts. In this case, the IT person may turn to the marketing manager for advice on the matter. Thus, the marketing manager is an influencer in the decision.

We commonly refer to some people as *centers of influence* or *opinion leaders* because of their power to influence others around them. These individuals are important to you, the persuader, because they can sway decision makers even though they have no formal decision-making role in the organization. For example, within the Republican realm of U.S. politics, William Kristol, editor of the *Weekly Standard*, is an important center of influence. Specifically, thanks to his frequent columns, media appearances, and access to top party leaders, he is widely considered a powerful shaper of Republicans' thinking. Among the opposing Democrats, Massachusetts senator Edward Kennedy plays a similar role. His position as the party's tribal elder and his long record of dedication to liberal causes give him substantial influence over fellow Democrats' policies and positions.

Harvard professor Michael Watkins refers to *influence networks* and suggests that persuaders map them out to better understand the complex relationships of influence among members of an organization.[3] Figure 6-1 depicts an influence map for a four-person team. The de-

FIGURE 6-1

Influence Map

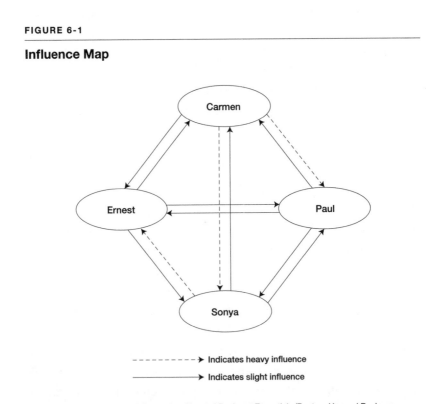

Source: Power, Influence, and Persuasion, Harvard Business Essentials (Boston: Harvard Business School Press, 2005), 66. Used with permission.

gree of influence between individuals is represented in the figure by the dotted and solid arrows connecting them. Dotted lines indicate heavy influence; solid lines, slight influence. Thus, Carmen exerts substantial influence over both Paul and Sonya. But these individuals, judging by their arrows, have less influence over Carmen.

An influence map can help you understand where to apply persuasion in a group setting. Using the example shown in figure 6-1, if you were trying to persuade Ernest about some matter, you might first test your ideas with Sonya, and possibly with Carmen. Sonya has strong influence on Ernest, whereas Carmen has a lesser degree.

Think for a moment about your workplace situation, including your superiors, peers, and subordinates. Sketch out an influence map like the one shown in figure 6-1. Now think about your current efforts to persuade the people in your map—whether you're advocating adoption of a new technology, creation of a new full-time position, or some other important goal. Have you targeted your persuasion campaigns at the right people? Have you concentrated on the final decision makers as well as taken into account individuals who might influence them in your favor? Appendix B contains tools that can help you be more effective in persuasion situations.

Now that you understand the roles of decision makers, stakeholders, and influencers, let's take a closer look at the situation facing Margaret—the benefits administration manager we met at the beginning of the chapter who wants her company to set up a vacation-donation policy. Margaret's situation demonstrates the importance of understanding precisely who your audience is.

For example, at Margaret's company, four individuals approve all new benefits policies: LaVonne, the HR director (Margaret's supervisor); Charles, the CEO; Timothy, the head of the legal department; and Frank, the CFO. Thus, they are the decision makers in this situation. But the web of influence among these three individuals is more complex than their formal power to approve or reject a policy. For example, Charles and Timothy have a history of frequently disagreeing on decisions because they have very different ideas about how to interpret certain policies. Timothy believes it's important to follow company policies to the letter, whereas Charles feels it's okay to interpret them more loosely. Because of these differences, there is often tension and some distrust between the two men. Margaret knows that it will be difficult for them to agree on her proposal.

In addition to these decision makers, Margaret needs to take into account the concerns of key stakeholders. Managers who supervise employees who frequently draw from the accumulating vacation "bank" constitute one key stakeholder group. They may have strong opinions about whether their employees should be allowed to take more time off than current policy stipulates. "We need these people to come in to work," they might say. These managers might not hesitate to go to LaVonne and try to persuade her to reject Margaret's proposal.

Employees themselves constitute another key stakeholder group. Some workers who might be in a position to donate vacation time to the bank might prefer to get paid for unused time off rather than give it away. A new vacation-donation policy might make them feel pressured to give up paid time off—and guilty if they don't contribute to the time bank. Again, these employees may express their concerns to LaVonne and their bosses, further influencing her decision about whether to support Margaret's proposal.

Another key stakeholder in this situation is Susan, the head of IT. If Margaret's proposal is approved, Susan may have to set up new record-keeping systems. If she's already feeling overloaded with work, the notion that she may be asked to take on additional responsibilities may worry her. And as it turns out, Susan is a good friend of Charles; thus, she's in a position to influence his decision about the proposed new policy.

Finally, Margaret's proposal faces additional challenges in the form of influencers. Specifically, Charles frequently asks Frank, the general manager of one of the company's divisions, for his insights on major decisions. That's because he views Frank as a thoughtful, well-rounded professional who knows how to weigh the various pros and cons of a situation. Though Frank doesn't have formal decision-making authority over benefits programs, any advice he gives Charles will be carefully considered and might influence Charles.

Clearly, Margaret faces a complex situation. Many currents of influence are at work among the decision makers, key stakeholders, and influencers who will have some impact on whether Margaret's proposal ultimately gets approved. She has a challenging road ahead of her.

Margaret's situation may strike you as similar to ones you've faced in *your* work—situations with a particular decision-making process, various stakeholders, and cross-currents of influence. How would *you* handle this one?

Analyze Audience Receptivity

After you've identified all the individuals who make up your true audience, it's time to analyze them. Audiences differ in what they may know about your proposal or idea, how interested they are in what you have to say, and how strongly they support your views—all of which influence their receptivity. To analyze audience receptivity, do the following:

- **Monitor reactions.** Look for signs of openness or resistance in e-mails and other formal or informal communications from your intended listeners. During meetings, observe how your listeners voice their concerns or express their opinions about topics related to your idea.

- **Assess body language.** Notice your listeners' tone of voice and body language during casual hallway conversations and other brief, informal exchanges. Does your intended audience seem interested in your ideas? Distracted by other concerns? Skeptical?

- **Talk with knowledgeable people.** Identify individuals who understand your audience members' moods and their expectations regarding important upcoming company developments. Ask these individuals for their thoughts about the likely receptivity to your idea. Ask what they and the key decision makers and stakeholders care about most, as well as what benefits they see in your idea.

Assess Categories of Receptivity

Audiences generally fall into one of five categories of receptivity: hostile, neutral, uninterested, uninformed, or supportive.

Hostile people disagree with you and may actively block you. To handle them, apply these practices:

- Use humor or a story to warm them up to you.

- Focus on areas of agreement.

- Demonstrate your expertise, and cite experts.

- Support statements with solid evidence.

- Stress that you're looking for a win–win outcome.

- Identify benefits that they would value.

It isn't always possible to win over people who start out in a hostile position. But you may be able to move them to a position of neutrality, the next best position for you. Once they become neutral, they at least will no longer strive to work against you.

Neutral people understand your position. They don't favor it, but they are not actively opposed. Your goal is to tilt these neutral people in your favor. In some cases, all that's needed is some convincing or careful application of charm. Some suggestions are:

- Spell out your proposition's benefits to these listeners.

- Keep it simple. Present only three clear, compelling points, backed by expert evidence, data, and concrete examples.

- Use stories, personal experiences, and anecdotes to appeal to their emotions.

- Point out the downside of *not* accepting your proposal.

- Discuss the alternatives that others might raise.

Uninterested people are informed about your subject but don't care about it. Like neutral listeners, uninterested listeners are not actively opposed to your position, but their lack of interest can block your success if a majority is required for your idea to win. Again, you must convert them to a position of actively supporting your idea. In many cases, the most powerful antidote to a lack of interest is to appeal to these individuals' self-interest. If you can demonstrate that your idea will improve their work lives, they may move out of the uninterested camp into the supportive one.

Uninformed people lack the information needed to become passionate, active supporters. In these cases, follow these guidelines:

- Establish your credibility by showcasing your experience or qualifications.

- Keep your presentation simple and straightforward; don't confuse these listeners with complex evaluations.

- Create an emotional link by sharing several personal anecdotes.

Supportive people already agree with you. Your goal is to keep them on your side and make them active agents of influence on your behalf. Here's how:

- Recharge their enthusiasm with vivid testimonials, and remind them of the benefits at stake.

- Help them anticipate and refute possible arguments from opponents.

- Hand out a detailed action plan with clear deadlines.

Determine Decision-Making Styles

To further boost your odds of persuading those who have the power to accept or reject your proposal, tailor your arguments to fit their decision-making style. People have distinct styles of decision making. In this section, we list four styles along with their characteristics and corresponding persuasion strategies.

How can you know which style your decision makers possess? In many cases you can observe a person's decision style in meetings and other workplace interactions. One of the best career moves you can make is to understand how all the people in your immediate workplace make decisions. Once you understand this, you'll enhance your ability to persuade them.

Here are the decision-making styles, and persuasion strategies you can use with them:

- **The thinker.** A thinker is a cerebral, logical, risk-averse person who needs lots of detail before making a decision. Strategy: Provide as much supporting data as possible to reduce risk. Persuade by using a fact-based approach.

- **The skeptic.** A skeptic will challenge every one of your points but in the end will make a decision based on emotions. Strategy: Establish as much credibility as possible. Invite the skeptic to challenge you, and play along with the game.

- **The follower.** This person takes his cues from the politically powerful. His thinking will converge with the majority. Strategy: Emphasize references and testimonials. Followers are very interested in how others have dealt with your issue. Understand who they follow or defer to; if you can get the support of those leaders, the followers will fall in line.

- **The controller.** A controller is unemotional and analytical in making decisions, highly wedded to her own ideas and less open to others. Strategy: Ensure that your argument is sound and well structured. Emphasize outcomes of value to this person.

Don't Forget About Politics

We'd all like to believe that a convincing argument is all we need to bring people around to our views. But the hard fact is, good arguments alone aren't enough. That's because politics plays a major role in many organizational decisions. Every company, division, and operating unit—like every state and city—has its share of political blocs that generally act in concert and in opposition to other blocs.

For example, if Al is in favor of a project, then his political allies, Sandra and Janis, will often take his side. Meanwhile, members of an opposing bloc are likely to automatically oppose the project because of their antipathy toward Al. Logical argument will take you only so far in an environment that is this highly charged with politics. The best you can do is to try to understand the issues for which politics comes into play, know what motivates people, and understand who's aligned with whom.

You've identified key stakeholders, decision makers, and influencers; analyzed your audience; and identified your decision makers' preferred styles. Now you're ready to take the next step: building a case that will capture your listeners' minds—if not their hearts.

Building a Case

Here is every persuader's dream. William has just wrapped up a meeting with three executive decision makers. The first executive initially had expressed little interest in William's proposal. The second had come to the meeting with a hostile attitude, and the third had an open mind. But by the end of the meeting, when they had to make the decision, the three looked at each other, shrugged their shoulders, and collectively said, "We can't argue with you about this proposal, William. It seems perfectly sensible. Let's do it."

This type of outcome is ideal—but very hard to attain. Why? A "perfectly sensible" case in favor of anything is difficult to create in a complex world of uncertainty and competing alternatives and interests. Even when a proposal's logic is unassailable, some decision makers will find reasons to resist it. "This would require too large a change for our people." Or "We have other alternatives." Or the objection that no one will admit to: "Your proposal would upset the status quo, from which I benefit immensely even though I contribute little to this organization." Other objections may have no plausible explanation other than what Mark Twain once referred to as "the cussedness of the human race."

Still, despite natural human resistance, building a rock-solid case remains the foundation of effective persuasion. In most cases, a rock-solid case has these characteristics:

- It is logical and consistent with facts and experience.

- It favorably addresses the interests of the parties you hope to persuade.

- It eliminates or neutralizes competing alternatives.

- It recognizes and deals with the politics of the situation.

- It comes with endorsements from objective and authoritative third parties.

When you make a case for something, is it this rock solid? If it isn't, use the preceding bullet points as a checklist for making it so. For example, suppose you'd like to see your organization adopt a "9/80" flextime program for employees. Through this program, eligible employees would be allowed to work eighty hours in nine workdays instead of the typical eighty hours in ten workdays (two weeks of eight-hour days). In many companies that have such a program, eligible employees work nine-hour days for nine days, then take every other Friday off.

You want to build a convincing case for adoption of the 9/80 program. Let's revisit the earlier checklist, this time adding examples of how you might craft a rock-solid case for 9/80:

- **Logical and consistent with facts and experience.** You gather statistics about employees' need for greater flexibility in their workday in order to balance work, family, and community responsibilities, as well as have time for outside interests. You also collect information showing that employee loyalty increases when people have more flexibility in their workdays.

- **Favorably addresses the interests of the parties you hope to persuade.** You prepare analyses of how increased employee loyalty leads to better customer service, which in turn boosts profits. Employees who have been with the company for a long time know the firm's products and customers better than new-comers and can provide continuity of service—which reassures customers and makes them want to keep doing business with your organization.

- **Eliminates or neutralizes competing alternatives.** You antici-pate that some decision makers might ask, "If flexibility is the key thing here, why don't we just let people come to work whenever they want, as long as they put in eight hours a day?" You prepare an explanation for why 9/80 is better than this basic flextime plan: letting people come to work whenever they want creates chaos. Since employees would be coming to work and leaving on many different schedules, the company would need to publish everyone's different schedule (7:00–3:00, 8:00–4:00, 9:00–5:00, and so forth). Arranging meetings would become a chore. With 9/80, people could instead work nine eight-hour days and take every other Friday off. Keeping track of people's out-of-the-office Fridays would be much easier than tracking daily flextime schedules.

- **Recognizes and deals with the politics of the situation.** You anticipate that some managers may complain about 9/80. Specifically, they may say, "My salaried employees have already been working more than eight-hour days. That's what salary is all about—they don't clock their hours. And they put in as much time as needed to get the job done. Now, with the 9/80 plan, they'll be out of the office every other Friday. I'll be getting less of their time than I used to." You prepare an argu-ment emphasizing the increased loyalty salaried employees will feel toward their managers and the company if employees have more flexible workweeks. To address these managers' concerns, you also brainstorm a suggestion: during crunch times, man-agers could require salaried employees to come in to work on a Friday that they were planning to take off—but also let them reschedule the Friday off for another week after project re-quirements or deadlines have been met.

- **Comes with endorsements from objective and authoritative third parties.** You gather testimonials from other companies in similar industries to yours that have initiated a 9/80 program and have achieved valuable results from it. You also provide information on the challenges these companies encountered in rolling out the program and the ways in which they surmounted those challenges.

Summing Up

In this chapter, you learned that:

- Persuasion is a process that enables a person or group to change or reinforce others' attitudes, opinions, or behaviors. It is essential for success in all relationships—personal and business alike.

- For managers, persuasion has become more necessary as the command-and-control nature of business gives way to employee participation, teams, and joint ventures.

- Persuasion has four elements: credibility, an understanding of the audience, a solid argument, and effective communication.

- Credibility is trust plus expertise. If you want to increase your credibility, increase the level of trust people have in you, your expertise, or both.

- People will perceive you as having expertise if you exercise sound judgment and demonstrate a history of successes.

- When you analyze the audience you hope to persuade, identify the decision makers and centers of influence, determine their likely receptivity, and learn how they make decisions.

- A rock-solid case is logical and consistent with facts and experience, favorably addresses the interests of the parties you hope to persuade, eliminates or neutralizes competing alternatives, recognizes and deals with the politics of the situation, and comes with endorsements from objective and authoritative third parties.

- The characteristics of a rock-solid case should be used whenever you aim to persuade.

Leveraging Chapter Insights: Critical Questions

- How would you assess your personal credibility? Do others perceive you as having valuable expertise? Do they trust you to follow through on what you say you'll do and to make smart decisions? What steps might you take to strengthen your credibility?

- Think of an idea for which you'd like others' support. Who are the people you need to convince of the idea's value? Which members of this audience are decision makers? Key stakeholders? Influencers? How might you gauge their receptivity to your idea? Depending on each audience member's receptivity, how might you adapt your pitch to win or secure their support?

- How will you present a rock-solid case for the idea you identified in the last question? What steps might you take to ensure that your case is logical and consistent with facts and experience, favorably addresses the interests of the parties you hope to persuade, eliminates or neutralizes competing alternatives, recognizes and deals with the politics of the situation, and comes with endorsements from objective and authoritative third parties?

CHAPTER SEVEN

Persuasion II

Winning Minds and Hearts

Key Topics Covered in This Chapter

- *Four approaches to appealing to the logic of your audience*

- *The role of emotions in decision making*

- *How language, vivid descriptions, metaphors, analogies, and stories can help your idea resonate with an audience*

- *The use of persuasion triggers*

I N T H E L A S T chapter, you prepared a rock-solid case for establishing a 9/80 flextime program in your company. You might think that the information you pulled together to build your case will be enough to persuade any fair-minded person to support your proposal. But information isn't everything in the realm of persuasion. Emotions, perceptions, and predispositions also play major roles in how people make decisions about new HR policies or programs and other important business matters. To persuade others to embrace your ideas, you thus need to address your listeners' *hearts* as well as their *minds*. This chapter focuses on strategies for winning both.[1]

Start with the Head

You can appeal to your listeners' reasoning power through several tactics:

- The way you structure your presentation

- The evidence you provide to back up your proposal

- The benefits you emphasize

- The words you use

    Let's take a closer look at each of these techniques.

Begin with the Right Structure

How do you decide what to say first, second, and so on in trying to win people to your point of view? Sometimes your assessment of your audience's receptivity (see chapter 6) will influence the structure you select. At other times, the subject matter will suggest the appropriate structure. You might also decide to use one structure to present your case to one audience (for example, a receptive audience) and another to present the same case to another audience (such as a skeptical audience). Consider the following examples of structures:

- **Problem-solution.** Describe a pressing problem, and then solve it by presenting a convincing solution. For example, "We're having trouble handling seasonal booms and busts in our business. During last year's holidays, we were short staffed in the customer service and fulfillment departments. By making more strategic use of contingent workers, we can expand and contract our labor pool more easily to accommodate shifting needs."

  Use the problem-solution structure with an uninterested audience or one that's uninformed about the problem.

- **Present both sides and a refutation.** To win over neutral or hostile audiences, argue both sides. First present your opponents' side, thereby showing that you accept the validity of their position and increasing their receptivity. Then refute their case point by point by challenging their evidence and disproving their arguments.

  For instance, "Jim, I agree with you that establishing a specialized retention manager will be expensive. We've already tightened our belts to the breaking point. But I ask you to consider the long-term payoff of this idea: by investing in retention of talented employees *now*, we'll save money later because we won't have to run as many recruiting ads or pay headhunters to replace defecting employees."

- **Motivational sequence.** Capture your audience's attention with a startling statistic, an anecdote, or a humorous story—and then identify a pressing need. Explain how your proposal will satisfy that need, and help listeners visualize the bright future in store if they adopt your proposal. Finally, tell your audience what actions you want them to take.

For example, "Seventy-five percent of large-scale change initiatives fail miserably. We need to beat these odds if we hope to stay competitive in a rapidly changing business world. The change-management training series I've recommended will help managers and employees master the skills required to implement large-scale change. Imagine this organization filled with people who welcome the challenge of major change rather than fear and resist it, and who commit themselves to making change happen. How do we get there? We can start by each making room in our schedules for participation in at least the introductory module of the series. I also need you to explain to your employees why education on change management is vital."

Use the motivational-sequence structure for supportive audiences.

How you begin and end your presentation is especially critical. Capture your audience's attention in the very beginning with a dynamic opening. Conclude with a call for action in which you clearly indicate what you want from your listeners.

Provide Compelling Evidence

The evidence you provide to support your proposal—testimonials, examples, statistics, and graphical evidence—can further strengthen your persuasiveness.

Testimonials enhance persuasiveness when they come from sources your audience considers expert and credible. For example, if you're advocating the adoption of a new HR technology, provide quotations from respected companies similar to yours that have adopted the technology and achieved excellent results with it: "According to Frank Quisling, VP of Human Resources for Cummins Manufacturing, Inc., 'adopting ClaimLynx software helped us cut our insurance-claims processing response time and costs in half. Our employees are now a lot happier, and so is our CFO.' "

Examples further capture people's attention by turning generalizations and abstractions into concrete proof. To illustrate, cite examples of what a proposed new HR technology can accomplish: "Each of [Cummins's] employees filing health-insurance claims has reported a reduction in response time of at least 35 percent within one month of installing and training people on ClaimLynx software."

Statistics become especially effective when you make them understandable and memorable. Consider these techniques:

- **Personalize cold, lifeless numbers.** "Four out of ten people in this room waited more than four months to receive their reimbursement checks after filing a health-insurance claim."

- **Cite eye-popping comparisons.** "Our main competitor is currently generating twice as many sales dollars per employee as we do. Can you imagine what our profit-sharing bonuses would look like if we doubled our sales per employee?"

- **Use graphics.** Slides, flip charts, videotapes, and product samples can help you impart evidence and capture people's attention. That's because visual information sticks with people. In fact, three-quarters of what people learn they acquire visually. But don't get carried away. Choose a medium that's appropriate to your message. If you employ a PowerPoint presentation, convey one concept per slide. Keep it simple and clear. When creating charts and tables, first determine the main trends or patterns you want to emphasize, and then take care not to distort or misrepresent information.

When carefully selected and compellingly presented, evidence in all its forms can win over your listeners through reason.

Spotlight the Benefits Your Listeners Value

The features of your idea—such as how a new software program you're advocating works—may interest some listeners. But its *benefits*—

how the idea will make their lives or work easier or more productive—will more strongly attract their attention. People who fail to answer their listeners' question "What's in it for me?" stand little chance of winning their minds. To understand this firsthand, consider table 7-1, which lists the features and benefits of a defined-contribution health plan. Which column do *you* find most appealing?

Each benefit may appeal to listeners on one of two primary levels of motivation: the desire for gain and the fear of loss.

- **Desire for gain.** A benefit may enable listeners to gain something they don't currently have—for example, money, time, popularity, possessions, or a good reputation.

- **Fear of loss.** A benefit may enable listeners to avoid losing something they currently have and value. Before the days of credit cards and automatic teller machines, American Express ran television ads showing a family vacation ruined when the hapless father lost his wallet. The message was clear: don't let this happen to you; carry our traveler's checks.

Research shows that the fear of loss motivates people far more powerfully than the prospect of gain. For example, the fear of losing money you already have will influence your decisions more than the

TABLE 7-1

A Defined-Contribution Health Plan: Features Versus Benefits

Features	Benefits
The plan offers twice as many participating HMOs, dental HMOs, and preferred provider organizations than the existing plan.	Employees have more control over which providers they can see and what services they receive.
The plan matches health-care demand more closely to price.	We contain health-care costs, because employees choose only the services they need.
Our company decides how much to contribute to the plan each year.	We don't get subjected to price shocks that come with skyrocketing health-care premiums.

prospect of gaining money you don't have. So think about which benefits your audience values most. Then develop a unique value proposition for your proposal by asking these questions:

- **What benefits does my proposal provide?** What will my audience gain? What will they avoid losing?

- **What evidence shows that these benefits are real?** Are there compelling and credible testimonials, examples, statistics, and graphical representations available to support this?

- **What makes my proposal unique?** What's different and unusual about my idea? Why should my audience accept my proposal and not others?

By spotlighting the unique advantages of your proposition, you convince listeners that your idea merits their serious consideration. See "Tips for Defining Your Unique Value Proposition" for additional recommendations.

Tips for Defining Your Unique Value Proposition

1. **Brainstorm the benefits.** Think about all the possible benefits of your proposition. What would your audience members gain, and what would they avoid losing, by accepting your proposition?

2. **Prioritize the benefits based on audience interests.** Of the benefits you've identified, which do you think your audience values most? Prioritize audience members' interests based on your understanding of their current problems, concerns, and values.

3. **Gather evidence showing that the high-priority benefits are real.** Collect compelling testimonials from credible

continued

sources showing that the benefits that matter most to the members of your audience are within their reach—if they accept your proposition. In addition, gather examples, statistics, and graphical representations that speak to the benefits of your proposition.

4. **Play up what makes your proposal unique.** Compare your idea against potential alternative propositions. What's different, unusual, and superior about your idea? Why should your audience accept your proposal and not others? Be ready to explain in succinct, compelling terms what makes your proposal better than others.

How well do you understand the people you're trying to persuade? Do you know who the decision makers are? Do you know what constitutes value in their minds? If you need help on this matter, make use of appendix B, which offers tools that can help you better understand your audience.

Select the Right Words

When persuasion is your aim, never underestimate the power of well-chosen words. The words you select can determine whether your listeners consider or dismiss your proposal. Choose affirmative, assertive, and responsible words that also foster collaboration and engender trust. Table 7-2 provides examples of effective and ineffective word selection.

Whenever possible—and only when appropriate to your audience—sprinkle attention-grabbing words, such as *easy, free, guaranteed, proven,* and *results,* throughout your persuasion communications. Emphasize key points with words such as *important, imperative, critical,* and *essential* without overdoing it. Despite their heavy use in the realm of sales, these words prove remarkably effective in persuasion efforts.

TABLE 7-2

Word Selection Matters

Type of Words Selected	Example of What to Say	Example of What Not to Say
Affirmative language communicates precisely what you expect to happen.	"*When* you finish that report, we'll celebrate by going out for a pizza."	"*If* you finish that report, we'll celebrate by going out for a pizza."
Assertive speech presents your arguments with confidence.	"Our project *needs* additional funding."	"I would *guess* that our project could use additional funding."
Accept responsibility for your circumstances.	"*I'll* have the person who is responsible phone you."	"I *can't* help you."
Win-win language fosters cooperation.	"That's a new approach. *Let's talk it through* to see where we end up."	"Maybe you should run some numbers, because *I don't see that working.*"
Phrasing can make people trust your integrity.	"*This is a much better deal* for you than the previous one."	"*To be perfectly honest,* I think this deal is perfect for you."

Source: Harvard ManageMentor. Adapted with permission.

Additional categories of words can compel people to consider your ideas, for different reasons. Consider these categories and examples:[2]

- **Imperative.** "Go for it," "Just do it," "Jump in," "Why wait?" "Let's move on this," "The time is ripe."

- **Highlighting results.** "We can *attain* these profits," "We'll *achieve* new market share," "We'll have an *advantage* over rivals."

- **Highlighting problem avoidance.** "You *won't have to* be short staffed again," "This will *solve* the problem we've been having," "We'll *get rid of* systems that have slowed us down," "Let's *fix* this."

- **Appealing to listener's power.** "*Only you* can decide about this proposal," "It's *up to you,*" "*Try out* the new technology and *decide what you think," "You will make quite an impact* on our bottom line if you use this system."

- **Evoking precision.** "This is *exactly* what we need," "It's *precisely* because we've ignored this opportunity that we've gotten into trouble."

- **Evoking excitement.** "I want to describe this *exciting* new program," "This *extraordinary* opportunity won't come again," "I found the advantages of this plan *mind-boggling.*"

- **Evoking community.** *"Together we* can turn this department around," *"All of us* can make a difference if we come to agreement on this," *"We* can make it happen," *"You won't be alone* in agreeing to give this a try," *"Let's share* in the responsibility and rewards that come with this opportunity."

- **Evoking the senses.** "Let me *show* you how this will work," "Can you *see* how this policy will play out?" *"Imagine* the day when we're known as the employer of choice," *"Listen* to these striking stories from managers who have adopted this tool," "This idea will enable us to *get in tune* with your workforce," "We can eliminate the *discord* that's been plaguing our executive team," "These facts are *solid,*" "The new system will *connect* employees to the company's mission," "Let's *grasp* this once-in-a-lifetime opportunity."

By structuring your presentation effectively, providing the best evidence, spotlighting your proposal's benefits, and selecting the right words, you boost your chances of winning your listeners' minds. Now let's see how to capture their hearts.

Don't Forget Your Audience's Heart

The most logical argument won't persuade people by itself—you also need to connect with your audience on an emotional level. In fact, emotions play a more powerful role in human decision making than facts, numbers, and a rational assessment of a proposal's benefits. Why? Experts cite several reasons:

- Emotion-evoking presentations—such as gripping stories—are more interesting and memorable than statistics and facts.

- Emotion tends to prompt behavioral changes more quickly than do logical appeals.

- Responding emotionally requires less effort than logically weighing the pros and cons of a presentation.

- Emotion-arousing arguments distract people from the speaker's intention to persuade.

In the most successful persuasive situations, people *first* accept the presenter's proposal unconsciously, based on their emotional response. Then they justify their decision based on a logical assessment of the facts, as in this example:

Mario, the manager of his company's marketing department, is having a rough day. First thing this morning, Anna, his best market researcher, gave notice—during one of the busiest times the department has experienced yet. Worse, this "defection" is just one in a series that has Mario increasingly concerned about turnover in his department. And Anna's resignation came out of the blue: Mario had no idea she was dissatisfied with her job. In fact, when he asked her why she was leaving, she gave a vague answer—something about "exploring other opportunities." Sitting at his desk with his head in his hands, he thinks about a particularly crucial project deadline that's looming—and wonders how in the world his group will manage it. He looks up at the clock on his office wall: Jeez, it's only ten o'clock, *he thinks to himself.* And my day is already shot.*

As Mario is dejectedly reviewing his situation, Beth, the director of HR, knocks on his door and asks if she can come in and talk for a minute. He wearily waves her to the visitor's chair next to his desk. "What's up?" he says.

"Well," answers Beth, "I wanted to get your thoughts about a new employee-retention study I'm proposing. I've taken a focused look at

*our turnover rates, including how they compare with our competitors',
and the news isn't good. We need to address this."*

*"I'm all over that," says Mario immediately. He tells Beth about
Anna's giving notice earlier this morning. "Frankly," he says, "I don't
know what's going on, but I've lost several good people, and I can't
afford to lose any more."*

*"You're not the only one who's experienced higher-than-usual
turnover," Beth tells him. "Of course, this study is going to require a lot
of support from management. We'll need you to pull together records
of previous employees, reconstruct what led to defections, and gather
honest, detailed feedback from current employees about their attitudes
toward the company. It'll take time, and I know everyone's busy."*

"Well, you can count me in," Mario says.

*Beth proceeds to pull out paperwork showing the retention rates
she's studied and analyses of competing companies' rates. She hands
these documents to Mario, along with several journal articles on the
high costs of turnover. "I thought you might be interested in learning
more of the details," she tells him. Mario nods and glances at the papers
in his hand. But he's not really looking at the numbers, nor does he
have any intention of taking time away from project deadlines to read
the articles Beth gave him. He was already sold on the idea of the
study the minute Beth described it to him. To him, it seems that Beth
and her idea could not have shown up at a better time. Already, he's
feeling a huge sense of relief that someone is offering to deal with his
problem. His day is suddenly looking a lot better.*

Emotions matter. For many people, feelings determine whether
they give a new idea a hearing at all. If a proposal appeals to them on
an emotional level, only then will they consider the accompanying
facts and figures. Often, they'll use the logical aspects of the presenter's case to justify their emotion-based decision.

One warning about emotions: some audiences want the facts
and will react negatively to any presentation that focuses solely on
emotional appeals. Consider the predicament your CEO and CFO
would be in if they made a presentation to a group of Wall Street
securities analysts and skipped the details of sales and earnings pro-

jections. If all they did was give a rosy description of how the company's products were changing people's lives for the better, most of the analysts would get up and leave the room.

Vivid Descriptions

Words that paint evocative images in people's minds deeply tap into listeners' emotions. For example, suppose you're the HR vice president at your firm, and you want to persuade your boss, the CEO, to allow some employees to work from their home offices several days each week. You anticipate that your boss will worry that this arrangement might reduce worker productivity and result in loss of control: "How will their managers know if they're working and not watching *Seinfeld* reruns?" he asks. To persuade him otherwise, vividly describe those employees working diligently from their home offices, free from the many distractions that permeate the office on a typical workday. Then contrast that picture with a description of employees being interrupted by frequent meetings and by well-meaning coworkers who stop by to chat. "How many meetings are nothing but time wasters?" you ask your CEO. "Most of them," he replies.

As you paint these images in your boss's mind, he begins experiencing two emotions: a desire for a more focused, industrious staff, and an aversion to the disruptive reality you've described. To seal the deal, you recognize his concern about loss of control. "In the end, it's results that count, isn't it?" you say. "If we give each home office worker clear goals with measurable deliverables, we'll know every week and every month who is doing the job and who isn't." With that assurance, the CEO agrees to a pilot program of home-based work for a handful of employees.

Metaphors

A *metaphor* is an imaginative way of describing something as something else—for example, "Time is money." *Organizing metaphors* are overarching worldviews that shape a person's everyday actions; for example, "Business is war." People reveal their organizing metaphors through the language they use. For example, a manager who sees business as war might say things like, "We can't concede ground," "We're being outflanked," or "We have to defend market share."

In some cases, persuasion requires changing a person's organizing metaphor. You can do this by replacing the existing metaphor with one that is more in line with what you aim to achieve; for example, you might attempt to replace "business as war" with "business as partnership." This metaphor focuses a business's efforts on building win–win relationships with key stakeholders rather than on crushing its competitors. You can achieve the same end by highlighting the weaknesses of your audience's worldview using their metaphor. For example, "By focusing on competitors instead of customer support, we've allowed our customer-satisfaction levels to fall."

Yet another approach to altering the organizing metaphor is through examples of other companies that have achieved success using your replacement metaphor, as in, "XYZ's sales have increased 18 percent since the company directed account managers to collaborate with the sales team."

Replacing someone's organizing metaphor is never easy; people cling tightly to their worldview. But by providing powerful evidence of the flaws in an existing metaphor and the veracity of the new one, you can persuade others to consider a different outlook.

Analogies

Analogies—comparisons that include the words *like* or *as*—enable you to relate a new idea to one that's already familiar to your audience. Analogies help your listeners understand and therefore accept a new idea. Analogies also engender feelings of familiarity, which many people find reassuring. Consider this example—an address given by a CEO to her workforce about the need to implement a large-scale change initiative:

> *Those of you who worked here at Gizmo Products in the 1980s surely remember the wrenching changes we had to make in abandoning our*

traditional hydraulic steering technology—a dying art—in favor of electronic steering systems. We had to give up decades of accumulated know-how and learn new, often unfamiliar, skills. Some people were unable to make the transition. Fortunately, the company made it through that transition and went on to become a leader in electronic steering. Today we face yet another transition that, like the previous one, will be just as difficult and every bit as critical to our future survival and success.

Incongruous analogies and those that use humor are all the more memorable. For example, when Benjamin Franklin once said, "Fish and visitors start to smell in three days," he delivered a vivid message of why people tire of visitors who outstay their welcome.

Stories

Stories also help make presentations come alive and drive messages home. They can accomplish the following:

- Grab listeners' attention with riveting plots and characters that audiences can relate to

- Simplify complex ideas and make them concrete

- Evoke powerful emotions among listeners

- Stay in your audience's mind long after the facts and complex details have been forgotten

As an example of successful storytelling, consider a product design manager who wants his team to generate more and better design ideas. His company is located in a region where many people have strong ties to the local community but where the economy is threatened by larger changes in the national economy. The manager evokes intense emotions in his team by telling the story of how competition from a major discount store destroyed businesses in his own hometown. He describes family businesses that have closed, childhood friends who had to move away in search of work, office buildings now vacant, and a crop of For Sale signs in what were once vibrant neighborhoods.

No one in the audience has been to that town, but all those in the room can picture it, empathize with the plight of its residents, and imagine how their own town could suffer a similar fate if businesses like theirs failed to prosper.

The manager concludes his story by challenging his team to "fight back" by coming up with ideas for "made here at home" products. His team is charged up by the presentation and responds with a number of practical and innovative design ideas that tap local strengths and talents.

Clearly, the language and imagery of stories can help you connect with your audience's emotions and win their hearts. But no matter how skillfully you use them to appeal to listeners' reason and emotions, you'll likely encounter at least some resistance to your proposals. Let's turn now to the topic of how to deal with resistance.

Overcoming Resistance

Even the most carefully thought-out proposal can meet with resistance. Resistance may have several sources. One person may be committed to a position that diametrically opposes yours. Another may disagree with your idea on technical grounds. Yet another may resist for philosophical reasons—for example, whereas you are advocating outsourcing some tasks, your opponent believes that companies should outsource as little as possible.

How do you move a resister to your point of view? The key lies in understanding the resister's position and then presenting the benefits of your idea in terms the resister values. The following guidelines can help.

Identify Resisters' Interests

Each of us has had unique experiences. These experiences have shaped our views of the world and have influenced how we respond to the ideas of others. If you encounter resistance after presenting a proposal, avoid the temptation to keep pressing your case. Instead, think about what may be driving a resister to disagree with you. Adapt your response accordingly.

For example, suppose you are seeking funding to redesign the employee surveys your company has been using to assess cultural attitudes, job satisfaction, and other indicators. You've begun questioning the design of the current surveys and the accuracy of the results, and you want to hire a survey-design firm to examine the current approach and suggest needed changes. The head of IT opposes your plan. She is concerned that if the study reveals the need to start gathering new kinds of data and overhauling existing survey-response databases, these changes will mean a lot of extra work for her. And she has a demanding project she wants to pursue. In her mind, this is a zero-sum game—one in which any gain for you will be a loss for her.

In this case, you might want to address her fears by demonstrating that you and she are not in fact in a zero-sum game. You might argue, for example, that improving the usefulness of employee surveys will actually save her time in the long run. If the company starts getting more accurate information from its surveys, it won't have to conduct as many in the future.

Understand Resisters' Emotions

Most resistance springs from two emotions: distrust and fear.

- **Distrust.** Your audience doesn't like you or what you represent. For example, perhaps the IT manager just described views HR professionals as overly emotional and unempirical. In this case, you should demonstrate qualities that the IT manager admires in others—such as analytical ability and attention to detail. At bottom, you must answer the question, "What are the personal characteristics that engender trust on the part of this person?"

- **Fear.** Your audience doesn't like your idea because of potential adverse consequences for them. For example, listeners may worry that your proposed restructuring will cost them their jobs. Allay those fears by addressing them directly. For example: "The proposed restructuring will affect many positions. There's no doubt about it. But none of you will lose your job as a result. Some jobs will disappear, but others will be created. There will be more than enough work for everyone in this division. Our plan provides for the skill training that some people will need to take on new responsibilities."

When you understand the emotions driving resistance, you can position yourself to address your listeners' fears and distrust.

Build Trust

One way to improve relationships is to build trust. You can build trust by listening carefully to resisters' concerns. By listening, you demonstrate that you understand and value your opponents as individuals and care about their concerns. When people feel that they've been heard and that their ideas are valued, they will become more open to considering your ideas. You can use the following techniques to demonstrate that you've heard what's on their minds.

- **Paraphrase.** Mirror the resister's points—for example, "So you're saying that you think I'm just advancing the party line." Paraphrasing prompts your listener to respond with comments such as, "Well, yes—I do." By getting the person to agree with you—even in this small way—you establish common ground, and that enables the individual to become more receptive to your ideas.

- **Clarify the issues.** Identify the resister's primary concerns— for example, "So what I hear you saying is that you have two main concerns. The first one you mentioned is probably the most important, right?" Again, you've established a level of understanding and agreement. You've also shown that you're capable of sorting out the vital issues.

Be Consistent in Verbal and Nonverbal Messages

Body language and tone of voice send a message. Make sure that these communication cues are compatible with the content of your spoken message. If they aren't, your resisters may view you as not credible or as conflicted about your position—and that can further stiffen their resistance and deepen their distrust. For example, to telegraph confidence in your position, check that your posture is upright, your hand gestures assertive, your gaze direct, and your voice loud enough to be heard, but not so loud as to intimidate or annoy your listeners. Many successful persuaders rehearse their nonverbal behaviors just as much as the text of their presentations.

Effective persuaders also recognize when they are becoming overly emotional or angry—two behaviors that are inappropriate and counterproductive in many persuasion situations. In most cases an emotional or angry attitude on your part will provoke the same among the people you hope to convince. That won't help your case. If this happens to you, recover by openly acknowledging and apologizing for such behaviors. Having the courage to publicly admit a mistake can help establish trust and credibility.

In practicing nonverbal signals before giving a presentation, carefully consider whether the signals are conveying the messages you intend. Keep in mind that no gesture or facial expression has a single, unvarying meaning. Indeed, the meaning of a particular gesture depends on cultural norms, personal style, and the physical setting. For example, if you cross your arms while giving a presentation, many experts might claim that you're sending a message of defiance. And indeed some of your listeners may interpret this behavior as defiance. But perhaps you're just cold.

The best you can do is to take cultural norms, physical setting, and other factors into account while considering the nonverbal signals you're using—and to try not to send a message you don't intend. Table 7-3 shows common nonverbal behaviors that many experts agree *may* communicate ineffective or damaging messages in some circumstances. Owing to the risk of miscommunication, it's probably best to avoid the behaviors shown in the table.

TABLE 7-3

What Are You *Really* Saying?

Nonverbal Signal	Possible Unintended Message
Putting your hands behind your back	"I can't be trusted."
Holding eye contact for more than a few seconds	"I'm flirting with you." "I'm threatening you."
"Steepling" your fingers	"I'm intellectually pretentious."
Hesitating before taking your turn to speak	"I'm trying to deceive you."
Tapping your foot or swinging your leg	"I'm nervous; I'd like nothing more than to get up and leave."
Touching your nose, cheek, or forehead, or stroking your chin	"I'm anxious." "I'm being dishonest." "I don't believe you."

Sources: Face-to-Face Communications for Clarity and Impact, The Results-Driven Manager Series (Boston: Harvard Business School Press, 2004), 73–94. *Harvard Business Review on Effective Communication* (Boston: Harvard Business School Press, 1999), 135. Used with permission.

Present Resisters' Viewpoints Before Presenting Your Own

If you suspect that you'll encounter resistance from members of your audience, prepare a two-sided argument: theirs and yours. During your presentation, acknowledge your resisters' arguments *first.* Doing so will disarm them by removing their opportunity to oppose you. Deprived of this opportunity, they'll be more open to discussing your idea and participating in solving the problem at hand.

Next, present your argument. Show clearly how it provides a more powerful solution than your opponents' proposal does. When possible, show how you've incorporated resisters' ideas, interests, values, and concerns into your solution.

Persuasion Triggers

People respond to persuasion in two ways: consciously and unconsciously. If someone's in a conscious mode, he or she might respond thoughtfully to a proposal—weighing its pros and cons and attending carefully to the logic and content of the message. In an ideal world, everyone would make decisions in this way. But in reality, many people don't have the time, information, or motivation to do so. Instead, they switch their decision making to an unconscious mode. This means they spend less time processing information. They make decisions based more on instinct than on reason. And they resort to persuasion triggers, or mental shortcuts, to decide how to respond to a proposal.[3] Consider this example:

> *Joe, a purchasing manager, must choose between a deal offered by Sue (a supplier's representative) and one offered by Bob. After going through the motions of weighing the advantages and disadvantages of the two, Joe chooses Sue's deal, even though it is inferior to Bob's. The reason? Joe likes Sue because she once did him a favor.*

Researchers have identified six persuasion triggers: contrast, liking, reciprocity, social proof, commitment and consistency, and authority. Let's examine each of these in turn.

Contrast

Judgment, like beauty, is always relative. So when people make decisions, they often look for a benchmark against which to assess the merits of their options. Consider this example:

> *The first candidate you interview for a marketing manager position seems far too expensive when she asks for a starting salary of $90,000. Her request looks much more reasonable when you contrast her against the only other suitable candidate, who wants $110,000.*

To activate the contrast trigger within your audience, create an "anchor" for judgments of the person you need to persuade. Many salespeople do this by first showing a potential customer the most expensive item in a product line. This makes a mid-priced item seem more affordable.

Liking

There's an old saying that we tend to like people who like us. Liking often emerges when people have something in common. Thus, a persuader can set the groundwork by becoming liked by the audience. We observe this in sales situations all the time. An effective salesperson tries to develop a sense of friendship with the potential customer before attempting to make a sale.

How might you activate the liking trigger? Create bonds with peers, supervisors, and direct reports by discovering common interests—whether it's a shared alma mater, a passion for white-water rafting, or a love of cooking. Demonstrate your liking for others by expressing genuine compliments and making positive statements about their ideas, solutions, abilities, and qualities.

Reciprocity

As we've seen in earlier chapters, many people feel a need to repay favors in kind. This almost instinctive wish to reciprocate exists in all societies. Marketers recognize and make use of this natural urge to reciprocate. For example, fund-raisers have found that when they enclose a small, seemingly insignificant gift in an envelope to potential donors, the volume of donations increases markedly.

To activate the reciprocity trigger, follow this rule: give before you ask. A small favor such as lending a fellow manager one of your staff members for a few days might be repaid fivefold when you later ask for that manager's support on an important project. In considering what to give, look for solutions that meet other individuals' needs as well as your own.

Take a moment to think about what you could give or freely lend to your coworkers or customers. Some of your time? Unused office space? Free samples? If you give these, you may be pleasantly surprised by what your colleagues give you in return.

Social Proof

Individuals are more likely to follow another person's lead if what he or she is advocating is popular, standard practice, or part of a trend. For example, during the typical public radio fund-raiser in the United States, the announcer will periodically mention the names of listeners who have just pledged their financial support: "Robert and

Elizabeth Harding of Salem, Massachusetts, have just become new members. So has Seth Browning of Lexington. So why don't you call now and join Seth and the Hardings to show your support for this station?" That is social proof in action.

How do you activate the social proof trigger? Remember the power of association: make a connection between yourself, your company, or your idea and individuals and organizations your audience admires. For example, "Over two-thirds of the *Fortune* 500 companies in the United States have adopted a flextime program like the one I'm proposing."

Use peer power to influence horizontally. For example, if you're trying to convince a group of skeptical peer managers about the merits of a new HR policy you're proposing, ask a respected manager in the organization who supports the initiative to speak up for it in a cross-functional meeting. You'll stand a better chance of persuading your colleagues with this person's testimony.

Commitment and Consistency

People are more likely to embrace a proposal if they've made a voluntary, public, and written commitment to doing so. For example, 92 percent of residents of an apartment complex who signed a petition supporting a new recreation center later donated money to the cause.

To activate the commitment and consistency trigger, make others' commitments voluntary, public, and documented. Suppose, for example, that you want to persuade an employee to submit payroll reports on time. To inspire this behavior, link the employee's commitment to timely reporting to a formal performance improvement plan that both of you sign.

If getting a commitment is difficult, start small. After you have activated this trigger, you can later turn a small commitment into a large one.

Authority

Many people are trained from childhood to automatically obey the requests of authority figures such as parents, doctors, and police.

Authority comes from a combination of position and its associated credentials. For example, your authority as an HR professional will be enhanced if you possess a graduate degree in human resources, have achieved certification as a Senior Professional in Human Resources (SPHR), or have management experience in departments outside HR. This is related to the notion of expertise cited earlier.

Appropriate clothing or other trappings of authority can also in-crease your chances of successful persuasion. Businesspeople who "power dress" for an important presentation improve the odds that their pitch will win their listeners' support.

To activate the authority trigger, make sure that the people you want to persuade are aware of the source of your authority. Use all the trappings of authority, such as appropriate clothing.

To extract the most persuasive power from the six triggers, use sev-eral in combination rather than one at a time.

Summing Up

In this chapter, you learned that:

- To persuade others, you need to address your listeners' logic and emotions.

- Logical appeals can be made through the way a presentation or argument is structured, the use of evidence, the benefits you offer, and the words you use.

- Emotions play a more powerful role in human decision making than facts, numbers, and a rational assessment of a proposal's benefits.

- Vivid descriptions, metaphors, analogies, and stories are among the tools you can use to appeal to the emotional side of an audience.

- To overcome resistance, begin by identifying the interests of the resister.

- Resistance is often motivated by distrust and fear, both of which can be overcome to some extent by an effective persuader.

- Some people resort to persuasion triggers, or mental shortcuts, while responding to persuasive appeals. Six of these triggers were explained here: contrast, liking, reciprocity, social proof, commitment and consistency, and authority. Use one or more of these to make your proposal more appealing to the emotional side of your audience.

Leveraging Chapter Insights: Critical Questions

- Think of an HR program, policy, or initiative you think your company should support. Consider the various audiences to whom you'll present your proposal. Depending on their likely receptivity, how might you best structure your presentation? For example, will you use the problem-solution frame? Will you present both sides and a refutation? Will you use the cause-and-effect frame? The motivation-sequence frame?

- What is the most compelling evidence you can gather to support your appeal?

- What words, descriptions, metaphors, analogies, and stories might you prepare to grab your audience's attention and appeal to their emotions?

- Which of your audience members are most likely to resist your idea? Why? How will you turn them around to your side of things? For example, will you ensure that your verbal and nonverbal messages are consistent? Will you address resisters' viewpoints before presenting your own?

- Which of the six persuasion triggers that you learned about in this chapter—contrast, liking, reciprocity, social proof, commitment and consistency, and authority—might you evoke to persuade your audience to adopt your idea? How would you go about activating those triggers?

CHAPTER EIGHT

The Knockout Presentation

A Timeless Tool of Persuasion

Key Topics Covered in This Chapter

- *Presentation structure—the Greek way*

- *Rhetorical devices*

- *Different learning styles of different listeners*

- *How to aim for the head and the heart*

- *How to combat stage fright*

ORMAL PRESENTATIONS are a powerful way to communicate your message about important HR programs and ideas and to persuade your audience to embrace your ideas. HR professionals use formal presentations to report progress to senior management, to sell their ideas to internal customers, to encourage adherence to a project goal or schedule, to explain the details of a proposal, and so forth. Although some of your presentations will aim to do nothing more than convey information, most will have the goal of influencing your audience or persuading listeners to accept your point of view.

This chapter gives you tools and techniques to create more persuasive presentations. It begins with a proven presentation structure—one that goes back to the time of the ancient Greeks. The next major section explains several rhetorical devices you can use to lend your presentation greater impact. Another section explains learning styles of typical audiences. If you understand these styles and know how to address them, your presentations will exert a more powerful impact on your listeners. Finally, the chapter offers practical advice about overcoming presentation anxiety.

Presentations: The Greek Way

In learning how to make a great presentation, take a cue from the people who did it first and did it well—the ancient Greeks.[1] The Athenian

Greeks developed a number of presentation techniques as they began their experiment with democratic government. The art of public speaking emerged from this experiment and the legal system that developed in its wake. Indeed, no one has managed to significantly improve upon the five-part Greek outline for a persuasive speech: introduction, narrative, argument, refutation, and conclusion. Some twenty-five centuries later, you can use the Greeks' insights to strengthen your own presentations. Let's examine each of these parts more closely.

The Introduction

Conventional wisdom tells us to divide a presentation or speech into three parts: tell the audience what you are going to say, then say it, and finally tell them what you just said. The Greeks did not subscribe to this approach. They found it predictable and boring—and many audiences over the ages have agreed. Listeners quickly figure out what you're up to, and once they do, they pay attention to one of the three parts of your presentation and ignore the rest.

The Greeks used the introduction to prepare their audience to hear the speech favorably. Here are a few of their strategies.

COMPLIMENT YOUR AUDIENCE. You can never go wrong complimenting your audience. For example:

> *It is a pleasure to work with managers like you, who have been instrumental in making our company an employer of choice.*

TALK ABOUT A PREVIOUS SPEAKER. If your presentation is one of a series, refer to a previous speaker who made a deep impression on the audience.

> *Jane moved us all with her eloquent discussion about our company's core values. Now, I'd like to talk with you about a subject I feel as strongly about as Jane feels about the company's values: the strategies and programs we are developing to train and retain a fully engaged workforce that will enable us to achieve our company's vision.*

TALK ABOUT THE EVENT. Draw attention to something that is special or unique about the event. Doing so heightens your listeners' interest and gives them a happy sense that the occasion is an important one. They'll listen more closely as a result.

This morning you will have the distinct privilege of meeting three of the most effective HR directors in our industry.

TALK ABOUT A MOMENT IN HISTORY. If you can put the time and date of the presentation into historical context, the audience will derive a greater sense of purpose and gravity.

Three years ago, I stood at this same podium and described to you the desperate shape our workforce was in. What a difference three years have made.

TALK ABOUT THE PLACE. The hall, the town, the state, or even the country where the presentation takes place is grist for the introductory mill.

This state, which has struggled so much in recent decades to reduce unemployment, has seen major improvements—thanks to companies like ours.

TALK ABOUT THE POINT OF THE SPEECH. An earlier chapter described framing as a valuable tool of influence. It is your privilege as the presenter to frame the topic and the context for the conversation you will have with the audience.

We're here today to talk about our company's health insurance costs over the past six months. Frankly, they've been skyrocketing. What really lies at the heart of the issue is a need to explore more radical solutions, and I'd like to spend a little time addressing that.

The Narrative

The essence of the narrative portion of your presentation is a story. Here you must get to the heart of the matter, whether it involves something you want your listeners to do or something you want to tell them about. If you don't find yourself phrasing what you have to say in terms of a story, rethink the material. Put the essence of your communication into a story that relates the facts in the way you wish your audience to understand them.

> *Before I describe the exciting things that are happening in the HR center today, let me take you back fifteen years and talk about the individual who set the course we are now following: Mark Johnson. Mark had more curiosity and innate inventiveness than any vice president of HR I've ever met. And he taught all who worked with him to think beyond what companies say they want from their workforce to the latent needs that many executives can't articulate. It is those latent needs that we are addressing with our current workforce-development programs.*

The Argument

In the argument part of your presentation, you present the proofs, or supporting logic, for your view. This section is probably the most important part of the presentation. Remember that audiences recall very little of what they hear. For this reason, keep your factual evidence to the necessary minimum and your main arguments to three or four at the most. Trying to present more than that will weaken your case. Why? Your audience will become exasperated and will conclude that you're trying to bolster a weak argument with every point you can think of.

Be sure to provide transitional comments throughout this section to help guide your audience through your line of thought.

> *There are several reasons why we need to improve our executive-development program. First, turnover among top-level executives is reaching unprecedented rates in our industry. Every time a CEO leaves a company, the entire organization is destabilized. Second, companies without a strong leadership pipeline are forced to hire from outside. An outsider isn't necessarily a poor choice. But failing to develop worthy internal candidates narrows the pool of options severely. Third, talented and ambitious managers today want to work for organizations that offer them a path of advancement. If we can't provide our best aspiring*

leaders with a clear shot at the top positions in this company, we'll lose them to competitors.

The Refutation

In the fourth section of the Greek speech model, you anticipate objections to your argument. (Note that this model differs from other models, in which speakers present and address objections earlier in their speech. Both models can be very effective.) The refutation section is particularly important when the subject is controversial. You must give a real hearing to opposing points of view, even if you intend to subsequently demolish them. Failure to address objections will cause your audience to complain that you never considered opposing points of view. The more explosive the topic, the more important it is to state those points of view and to do so early in the refutation.

You can handle the refutation in two ways:

1. **Answer anticipated rebuttals to your own arguments.** "People have told me to forget about building product lines around new technologies. 'Business is good,' they say, 'so why change anything?' Business was also good for record manufacturers before the era of tapes and CDs. But one day those companies woke up and found that technological change had left them behind—and almost every one of them has disappeared. We are confronting a similar possibility today."

2. **Take the opportunity to reject your opponents' arguments.** Again, this tactic is essential for highly controversial topics. "To those who say that the data storage system I've been advocating will simply cannibalize our current storage system business, I say this: wouldn't you rather that we did it than have someone else do it to us?"

The Conclusion

Your conclusion should not summarize your arguments; rather, it should appeal to your listeners for their understanding, their action, and their approval—whatever it is you want them to do or think. So don't fall into the trap of telling your audience what you've already said. Summing up is a surefire way to kill any enthusiasm your presentation may have fired up. Instead of summarizing, tell your listeners what you want them to think or do.

As you leave here today, do so with the confidence that the training programs we've put in place have the strongest success in the industry and have won the approval of the top accrediting organizations.

While deciding how to construct your presentation, it's helpful to jot down an outline of your strategy, based on the five-part structure we've just explored. See "Putting It All Together" for a sample outline that you might prepare before giving a presentation intended to persuade executives to approve a new methodology for matching employee skills to the company's needs.

Putting It All Together

You've long known that your company needs to do a better job of matching employees' skills to long-term corporate strategy. Now you want to make a convincing case for an initiative that will enable your organization to define needed skills in specific terms and match them correctly to company needs. You've decided to use the five-part structure that the ancient Greeks developed. Here's how you might outline the content of your presentation:

- **Introduction.** I want to talk with you today about what defines a high-performance workforce for our company— and why it's become more important than ever.

- **Narrative.** Not too long ago, a company's most competitive assets were tangible—they consisted of the organization's factories, machinery, and other physical resources. But today, in the Age of Knowledge, an organization's ability to compete

continued

stems far more from the quality of its workforce than the
quality of its physical assets. For that reason, it's essential that
we start clearly identifying the skills and knowledge our
employees need to carry out our competitive strategy, and
matching those skills and knowledge to each role in the
company. We haven't paid attention to this clarity in the past,
and this neglect has hurt us.

- **Argument.** As competition in our industry stiffens, the urgency to leverage our workforce grows. The quality of our workforce can give us a huge advantage in an increasingly tough business arena. What does a high-quality workforce look like? Every employee has the skills and knowledge he or she needs to help carry out our own high-level corporate strategy.

- **Refutation.** I know that some of you have concerns about the amount of time and money that overhauling our skills analysis and matching processes will require. Yes, this initiative will need an up-front investment from everyone—especially your time. You've already got a lot on your plates. But by taking the time now to create consistent definitions of needed skills and corresponding job descriptions, you'll save time in the long run—because you won't have to redeploy employees who don't bring the right skills to the table. The new process may also mean some layoffs or termination of employees who cannot provide the needed skills. This is always painful, and we'll do everything we can to provide terminated employees with the support and resources they need to exit with dignity and find new employment.

- **Conclusion.** As you think over what I've said today, keep in mind that only you have the power to ensure your employees have what it takes to make us a top competitor in our industry. Start thinking about how your unit aligns behind

> our corporate strategy and what skills your people must possess in order for your unit to carry out its mission. Ask yourself if your team has those skills. If not, what changes can you make to better match your people's skills and knowledge with their roles in your unit?
>
> Of course, you'll flesh out such notes as you continue to prepare for and rehearse your presentation. But creating an outline can help you experiment with and familiarize yourself with the overall structure of your case. That familiarity in turn will help you remember the content and deliver it smoothly and confidently.

Rhetorical Devices

The ancient Greeks didn't simply develop a five-part structure for making a presentation. They also developed rhetorical devices for connecting with audiences—devices that remain highly effective today. These include parallel structure, triads, antithesis, and rhetorical questions. You can use these devices to make your presentations more persuasive.

Parallel Structure

Parallel structure uses sentence elements that are alike in both function and construction. Parallel structure is especially useful in presentations because the repetition of language structure helps audiences hear and remember what you have to say. Consider Churchill's speech on Dunkirk to the House of Commons in June 1940:

> *We shall not flag or fail. We shall go on to the end. We shall fight in France. We shall fight on the seas and oceans. We shall fight with growing confidence and growing strength in the air. We shall defend our island, whatever the cost may be. We shall fight on the beaches. We shall fight on the landing grounds. We shall fight in the fields and in the streets. We shall fight in the hills; we shall never surrender.*

You can use similar language structure to good effect in persuading people to accept a course of action: "We will work hard. We will work smart. We will create a better future for our company and for ourselves."

Triads

The Greeks noticed early on that people are attracted to lists of three items. Whether you call it the Rule of Threes or simply a *triad*, a group of three seems to our minds complete and satisfying. No one is quite sure why. The end of Martin Luther King's famous "I Have a Dream" speech illustrates the use of triads. Note the three groups King cites as "God's children":

> *When we let freedom ring, when we let it ring from every village and every hamlet, from every state and every city, we will be able to speed up that day when all of God's children, black men and white men, Jews and Gentiles, Protestants and Catholics, will be able to join hands and sing in the words of the old Negro spiritual, "Free at last! Free at last! Thank God Almighty, we are free at last!"*

You can use triads to good effect in any number of business presentations:

> *This new employee referral program will reduce our advertising costs, shorten the average time required to fill positions, and increase the quality of new hires.*

Here's another example:

> *The new strategy will work if we do our job as managers. That means articulating our goals, making sure that every employee understands how his or her job fits with the strategy, and aligning rewards with the right behavior at every level.*

Antithesis

In rhetoric, *antithesis* is the placing of a sentence or one of its parts in opposition to another to capture the listener's attention or to evoke a strong response. Consider, for example, the motto of New Hampshire: Live Free or Die.

Antithesis is rarely used today, even though it is an elegant form of expression and one that people remember vividly. Consider President John F. Kennedy's inaugural address in January 1961. The entire speech was laced with antithesis, but the passage toward the end of the speech had particular potency because it spoke directly to the audience:

> *And so, my fellow Americans, ask not what your country can do for you; ask what you can do for your country.*

Because of its dramatic effect, antithesis is less available to the typical business speaker. Still, you may find opportunities:

> *The choice is ours. We can live with the defender's dilemma, or we can grasp the innovator's advantage.*

Rhetorical Questions

Rhetorical questions are questions asked for the sole purpose of producing an effect. The speaker does not expect the question to be answered—least of all by the audience. Rhetorical questions draw listeners into the topic by calling for answers, even if those answers are not uttered. Consider Patrick Henry's famous speech of March 1775, only one month before the initial armed clashes of the American revolution:

> *Gentlemen may cry, "Peace! Peace!" but there is no peace. The war is actually begun! The next gale that sweeps from the north will bring to our ears the clash of resounding arms! Our brethren are already in the field! Why stand we here idle? What is it that gentlemen wish? What would they have? Is life so dear, or peace so sweet, as to be purchased at the price of chains and slavery?*

Having posed his rhetorical questions, Henry answered them in the strongest terms:

> *Forbid it, Almighty God! I know not what course others may take, but as for me, give me liberty, or give me death!*

Note the antithesis in Patrick Henry's last sentence.

As a businessperson, you have ample opportunities for posing rhetorical questions and for stating your reply to them. Consider this example:

> *If we continue following the same ineffective strategy, this company can expect the same result: shrinking market share and declining profitabil-ity. Do you want to work for a company like that? Are you comfortable with mediocrity? I doubt it. That's why I have offered this plan, and why I'm here today to ask for your support.*

Regardless of the techniques you use while delivering a presentation, always remain aware of the impact your words and delivery are having on your audience. See "Tips for Speaking with Impact" for helpful guidelines.

Tips for Speaking with Impact

In making a persuasive presentation, it's not only *what* you say that matters. *How* you say it exerts a powerful impact on your audience. So make the most of these tips:

- **Vary your speaking pace to suit your purpose.** Speaking fast helps you excite and energize your audience, whereas a slow pace creates a mood of anticipation. For most of your presentation, the best pace is to speak slowly enough for listeners to follow but quickly enough to sustain their interest.

- **Use a low pitch to project authority.** Many people inter-pret a low-pitched voice as authoritative and influential. Similarly, completing a sentence with a downward inflec-tion (a lowering of pitch) communicates confidence and certainty.

- **Control loudness.** Speak loudly enough to be heard but not so loudly as to irritate or offend listeners. To dramatize a moment, try lowering the volume of your voice. Stress important words and phrases with a bit more loudness.

- **Sharpen your articulation.** Clear, crisply articulated words and phrases convey confidence and competence. Such enunciation is also easy to follow.

- **Use pauses for impact.** A correctly timed pause can help you emphasize information and create a desired mood in your audience. It can also alert your audience that a special point is coming. Pause just before the point you want to emphasize— for example, "Our sales increased . . . twenty-five percent this year." Count "one, two, three" to yourself while pausing, and maintain eye contact with your listeners during the pause.

Different Listeners—Different Learning Styles

Another point to remember as you develop and present your ideas is that different audience members are likely to have different primary styles of learning.[2] You may be familiar with the three learning styles, typically referred to as visual, auditory, and kinesthetic. Most people are strong in one of these styles and weaker in the others.

- **Visual learners.** These learners respond best to pictures, graphs, and other visual stimuli. Research shows that 30 to 40 percent of people are visual learners.

- **Auditory learners.** As you may have guessed, these people are more responsive to words and other sounds. An estimated 20 to 30 percent of the population are auditory learners.

- **Kinesthetic learners.** These people are most engaged by physical activities: handling a prototype, working at a laboratory bench, or watching a presenter who moves around, mingles with the audience, or uses props. Some 30 to 50 percent of people are kinesthetic learners.

To get the attention of these different types of learners and persuade them to respond to your message, couch your presentation in their learning modes.

Adapting your presentation to different learning styles is easier said than done, because you can never be certain about the preferred style of a particular audience. Moreover, any audience is bound to contain a mixture of visual, auditory, and kinesthetic learners. How should you deal with the uncertainty? Provide something for everyone—a blend of visual, auditory, and kinesthetic appeals.

To appreciate the need for a blend of appeals, consider a typical business presentation. One of your colleagues is reporting her department's financial results for the previous quarter. She stands in front of the group, turns on an overhead projector or her computer, and cues up the first slide. A sea of words and numbers assaults your weary eyes. She then launches into reading every word on the screen. You shift in your chair, trying to get comfortable. As slide after slide winks by and your colleague continues to drone on in a flat voice, you gradually sink into a stupor. At the end, you shake yourself awake and exit the meeting room wondering, "What was that about?"

Here's how your colleague might appeal to the three learning styles to transform this doleful scene into a successful one.

- **Add a dose of visual learning.** Like most presenters, your colleague thinks she has appealed to visual learners by using slides. But most business slides are covered border to border with words. What visual learners need are pictures—preferably, simple ones. So connect your key concepts visually to angles, circles, squares, and the like. Don't get fancy—it's simply not necessary, and it doesn't promote learning. In addition to pictures, consider using tables and other illustrations for variety, but keep in mind that simpler is usually better.

- **Cue up your auditory learners.** You reach auditory learners through talk—but certain kinds of talk work better than others. Storytelling is one. Parables and anecdotes appeal to auditory learners and often remain in their minds long after your presentation has ended. In addition, you can employ discussion groups, debates, question-and-answer sessions, and the like—anything interactive that will get you talking in ways more connected to a story than the usual discursive style of business presentation.

- **Add liveliness through kinesthetic learning.** Kinesthetic learners may be the most neglected people at business presentations. Much of what goes on in the business world appeals to the head and not the body, and presentations are rarely exceptions to this dismal rule. The key here is to get your listeners to *do* something. Get them involved early and often through role-playing, games, working with models, even creating charts and physical representations of what you want them to learn. For example, you can increase your listeners' energy enormously at the opening of a speech simply by having them stand up and shout something appropriate or fun. It's corny, but it works. That's because you have appealed to the kinesthetics in the audience.

Use all three of these learning modes in a presentation, and you'll capture your audience's attention and ensure that they remember your ideas.

Visual images containing text and graphics have become a standard feature in formal presentations, so it is imperative that you master them. When used judiciously, visual images can get key points across and make them memorable. Used without thought or discipline, however, these tools can confuse or bore your audience, diminishing the impact of your entire presentation. To learn how to make the most of visual aids, see appendix D, "Commonsense Rules for Presentation Visuals."

Aim for the Head *and* the Heart

We have already addressed the subject of audience emotions in chapter 7's discussion of persuasion. But let's revisit it here in the context of formal presentations.

Our business culture has a decided slant toward the analytical and cerebral. So it's not surprising that many presenters concentrate on the logic of their arguments and quantitative supporting evidence. Presentations either lack an emotional component or, if the component is there, bury it under a mountain of facts and figures. In making a case for a new pay-for-performance program, for example, you will inevitably roll out lots of data on employee productivity, payroll costs, and other numerical fireworks. All this information aims for the head.

Many business issues, however, have unstated personal and emotional components. These components may exert substantial power over listeners. Consider the pay-for-performance program. On the surface, it's all about potential productivity, cost estimates, and fit with company strategy. Beneath the surface, however, the program may affect individual listeners in important ways, including the following:

- **As a threat.** "If that program is adopted, I may make less money than before."

- **As an opportunity to benefit personally.** "If this thing works, our annual bonuses will triple. I could help my kids pay off their college loans, or I could retire early."

- **As a change in the workplace.** "If it works as planned, that new program would make a big difference around here. We wouldn't always be worried about deadwood getting away with not contributing anything. People would know that they were being rewarded for a job well done."

A good presentation recognizes these emotion-laden concerns. The presenter speaks to the head *and* the heart. In doing so, you engage listeners at a deeper level. Consequently, after you've presented the intellectual side of your story, shift to its deeper personal meaning for the audience. Use personal pronouns to signal your shift from cold-blooded objectivity:

That concludes my presentation of the benefits and cost estimates for the proposed pay-for-performance program. I have confidence in those estimates and the long-term workforce productivity they point to. I believe, too, that this program has the power to change our company in fundamental ways—and for the better. If you're tired of seeing mediocrity get rewarded in this company, this program will restore your pride in what we stand for: top-notch performance. If you're tired of working hard and not earning the recognition you deserve, this program will resurrect your trust in the company's commitment to fairness.

Did you notice all the personal pronouns in that ending: *we, you, you're, our*? Don't lay it on too thick, but speak to the hearts of your listeners if it's appropriate to the situation and if you want to make a real impression.

Be Prepared to Answer Questions

Questions taken from your audience can help you further engage listeners and drive your persuasive points home. The best time for Q&A is at the very end of your presentation; this strategy allows you to complete your delivery as planned. It's also a good idea to let your audience know at the very beginning that you'll provide time for questions at the end. Doing so has two benefits: it prevents unwanted interruptions, and it ensures that listeners will have heard your entire presentation before they ask questions. Taking questions during the presentation also has its advantages. For example, it keeps people engaged and gives you feedback about how well they understand your message. But this approach may cause you to lose control of your talk.

Anticipate Likely Questions

Q&A entails risk for the presenter. If you must repeatedly say, "I don't know," "I'm not sure," or "I'll have to get back to you on that," the credibility of your presentation will suffer. You can reduce that risk by anticipating and developing answers for likely questions as part of your presentation preparation.

To anticipate likely questions, take a moment to understand your audience. Who will attend the presentation? Why are they coming? What are their concerns? How is your presentation likely to strike them? Which of your arguments conflict with what they currently believe? For example, if your presentation concerns the adoption of a new employee dental insurance plan, you'll want to have answers to specific and predictable questions at the ready (unless you cover these details in the body of the presentation):

- How much will employees have to contribute to the plan each month?

- Is there an annual deductible that employees must pay before the plan benefits kick in?

- Does the plan cover orthodontia?

- Are all family members automatically covered by the plan?

- If not, what is the cost of additional coverage?

It's impossible to anticipate and prepare for every question that may come your way. For this reason, brace yourself to think on your feet and to redirect questions. For these tasks, you have four tools: feedback, paraphrasing, clarification, and empathy.[3]

Give Feedback

Feedback is a form of two-way communication. A person says something, and you respond, giving your reaction to what was said, as in the following example.

> You're a senior manager responsible for developing a new software product that is late to market and far over budget. You've been asked to rally the troops and urge them on. You finish your talk with some stirring words about pioneers and landing on the moon. You hope that your remarks didn't sound too clichéd. Now it's time for Q&A. The first question comes from a person in the back of the room.
> "Pardon my skepticism, but we've been hearing this same stuff from senior management for months now. We don't need another pep talk. What we really need is more help and a lot less red tape."

This is the question you most feared. You begin to think that your speech has had no impact. You take a deep breath, and respond. "The fact is, we're committed to getting you more help. We're struggling to hire qualified people. But as you know, qualified software developers are very hard to find right now. And we don't want to create more problems by hiring second-best personnel who will make your work more difficult. If you know of any qualified software developers, please get in touch with Human Resources and give the department this information.

"As for red tape, we'd like to think that we eliminated most of it when we set you up in a separate building and organized the project into self-managing teams. Next question?"

On the surface, in this example, you've responded to each of the points raised by the questioner. And yet your response may do little to cure the questioner's negative attitude—an attitude that others may share. You could have done more, as demonstrated next.

Paraphrase the Question

Paraphrasing the question is a technique for mirroring the questioner's points. It indicates that you are listening and interested in what that person has to say. Let's look at how this tool works in the same example:

So what you're saying is that I'm just giving the party line when what you really need is more help and less red tape. Is that right?

The questioner's likely response is "Yes." Now the hostile questioner is agreeing with you. You can then go on to give your feedback, in the words used in the case study example—but this time you'll have a more receptive listener. Yet there are even better ways to respond.

Clarify the Issues

In clarifying the issues, you work a little harder with the questioner's words to identify his real concerns. Let's see how that would happen here:

So what I hear you saying is that you see two key problems: too few people and too much red tape. The first is probably the most important. Is that right?

Again, you've established a level of agreement with the questioner. By clarifying, however, you've gone a step further. You've shown the audience that you're genuinely interested in trying to sort out the vital issues. In this way, you keep better control of the Q&A session.

Demonstrate Empathy

Empathy is the ability to identify with or vicariously experience the thoughts or feelings of others. Anything you can do during a presen-

Tips for Handling Q&A

The following tips can help you and your listeners get the full benefit from your presentation.

- Make a clear transition to the Q&A session.

- If the audience is larger than just a few people, repeat the question for the audience to hear.

- Maintain control of Q&A by rephrasing the question and giving the answer to the whole group and not only to the questioner.

- If you don't know the answer to a question, direct the person to a source for the answer, or offer to get the answer later.

- If you get a hostile question, find out the reasons for the hostility. Acknowledge valid points, and reject those that are not accurate. Then politely move on.

- Don't allow a long-winded questioner to monopolize the Q&A session. Say, "So that other people get a chance to talk, let me stop you there and see if I can answer the question."

tation to demonstrate genuine empathy will improve your standing with the audience and will help neutralize any subliminal hostility. As former U.S. president Bill Clinton was fond of stating, "I feel your pain." Members of the audience who sense genuine empathy will think, "She understands our problems" or "She's really one of us. We can trust her." Trust opens the door to persuasion.

The Q&A session is one of the obvious places where you can demonstrate empathy with your audience, as in our software project example.

> *I recognize the hardship that long hours and too few helping hands have caused people on your team. One person told me just last week about how she had to miss her daughter's first soccer game. I have young kids, too, so I know how she must feel. That's why we're sending HR people to every software job fair and doing everything we can to find qualified people who can lighten your load.*

"Tips for Handling Q&A" provides additional suggestions.

Overcome Presentation Anxiety

If the notion of giving a talk in front of a small or large group makes you nervous, you're not alone. Even accomplished public speakers often feel at least some degree of anxiety before delivering a presentation. Though stage fright is common, that doesn't mean you shouldn't find ways to tackle it. Ignore it, and you risk stumbling badly during your delivery.

Luckily, experts have identified numerous helpful strategies for combating stage fright.[4] The most powerful antidote to anxiety? Preparation. The more thoroughly prepared you are, the less nervous you'll feel while delivering your presentation. Consider the following preparation tactics:

- **Know your topic.** Your listeners will know if you're bluffing, and they'll begin questioning your credibility. To combat this, thoroughly familiarize yourself with the topic of your presentation.

Conduct enough research and talk with enough experts to get to the point where you feel confident that *you're* the expert.

- **Know your audience.** Acquaint yourself with your audience beforehand, including talking with a few members, asking what interests them, and finding out what they know about the topic of your talk.

- **Know the setting.** Before your presentation, stroll through the setting to familiarize yourself with it. Make sure the room's acoustics are good and that any audiovisual equipment you'll be using is in place and functioning properly.

- **Prepare more material than you think you'll use.** If you're giving a five-minute talk, develop enough material for fifteen minutes. It's better to pare down than to run out of things to say.

- **Imagine questions people might ask.** As noted earlier, anticipating questions your listeners might have about your topic is an excellent way to prepare. While rehearsing your speech, develop and practice responses to anticipated questions. Either work your responses into your delivery or hold them for the Q&A session at the end of your presentation. Even if the expected questions never arise, preparing yourself to answer them will help you feel more confident.

- **Memorize the first minute of your presentation.** Most public speakers experience the most intense anxiety during the beginning of their presentation. For this reason, memorizing the opening section of your talk can help you feel more comfortable as you begin your delivery. You may also want to memorize the last section of your presentation so as to conclude with confidence and conviction.

Even if you've taken steps to control your feelings of nervousness, you may still experience physical symptoms of anxiety during a presentation. Manage these through simple techniques. For example, if your hands tend to shake when you're nervous, place them authoritatively on the lectern. Put notes on a clipboard to prevent paper-rattling. If you blush when anxious, wear a scarf or a turtleneck to hide the flushing—which often starts at the chest and works its way up your neck.

Redirecting your attention from yourself to your audience can also vastly help you manage your anxiety. During your presentation, make eye contact and talk directly to individual listeners. Smile and nod your head as you address each listener in turn; you'll likely see them smile and nod as well.

For a quick-reference guide to reducing anxiety about public speaking, see "Twenty Strategies for Reducing Stage Fright."

Twenty Strategies for Reducing Stage Fright

1. Remind yourself that your listeners want you to do well.

2. Believe that you know more about your subject than your audience does.

3. Familiarize yourself with the physical setting of your presentation before you deliver it.

4. Get to know some members of your audience before you speak.

5. Choose a presentation topic you know something about.

6. Prepare thoroughly for delivery of your presentation.

7. Anticipate questions listeners might ask.

8. Memorize the first and last sections of your presentation.

9. Focus on your audience, not yourself.

10. Don't practice in front of a mirror.

11. Never tell the audience you're nervous.

12. View physical symptoms as positive excitement, not negative energy.

continued

13. Talk positively about your presentation to yourself.

14. Turn your nervous energy into something positive.

15. Abandon rigid rules about public speaking.

16. Tell yourself it's okay to make changes and adapt your delivery during your presentation.

17. Remind yourself that if things don't go well, it's not the end of the world.

18. Remember that even very nervous speakers usually appear calm to their audience.

19. Believe compliments on your delivery.

20. Anticipate problems and devise solutions ahead of time.

SOURCE: John Daly and Isa Engleberg, "Coping with Stage Fright," *Presentations That Motivate and Persuade,* The Results-Driven Manager Series (Boston: Harvard Business School Press, 2004), 55. Used with permission.

Aim for Continuous Improvement

Like any other activity, a presentation results from a process that converts inputs (your ideas, information, and arguments) to outputs (what your audience sees and hears). And like any other process, the presentation process can be improved.

Process improvement—whether it has to do with making automobiles or making persuasive presentations to the board of directors—drives quality. The quality movement that swept through manufacturing in the 1980s and through services in succeeding years has taught us that if we want a higher level of output quality, we should look first to the output itself. Is it up to standard, or are there measurable defects? When defects are found, we must trace them back to their root causes. Once we understand these causes, we can take corrective action.

Follow this same approach after every presentation. If you take the time to objectively evaluate a presentation after the fact (or after a rehearsal), you will enable yourself to pinpoint the root causes of poor performance. For example, you may find that cluttered over-heads, weak opening remarks, inept attempts at humor, or something else has led to a less-than-effective delivery. When you've identified the problems, do something about them as you prepare for your next presentation. In that way, you'll never make the same mistake twice.

One of the best ways to evaluate your performance and to pin-point areas for improvement is to videotape and review each of your presentations or rehearsals for a particular talk. If videotaping isn't possible, ask one or more helpful colleagues to note what went well and what went poorly during one of your presentations. An after-action review of the tape or the colleagues' notes will put you in touch with the best and worst of your presentation skills. If you work at continuous improvement, your presentations will become increas-ingly effective—and your standing in the organization will rise.

Table 8-1 lists some common presentation pitfalls to watch for as you continuously evaluate your public speaking abilities, and of-fers suggestions for avoiding them.

TABLE 8-1

Avoiding Common Presentation Pitfalls

Instead of . . .	. . . Try this instead
Reading from a script (which bores your audience)	Look up and establish a personal connection with your audience.
Hiding behind a podium	Walk around it so your audience can see you and read your body language.
Running over the allotted time for your presentation	Ask a trusted colleague in your audience to give you a subtle signal that you have five minutes left, and then one minute left, for your presentation.
Going off on a tangent with a long anecdote	Make sure all anecdotes have some connection to your main argument.
Assuming that you know your audience	Use questions—such as "Does everyone here under-stand what single-entry accounting is?"—to assess listeners' familiarity with your topic and level of knowledge.

(continued)

TABLE 8-1 (continued)

Avoiding Common Presentation Pitfalls

Instead of . . .	. . . Try this instead
Jumping into facts and figures at the beginning of your delivery	Grab listeners' attention by briefly describing the problem at hand in vivid, compelling terms or offering a gripping anecdote.
Leaving it up to your audience to figure out where your presentation is going	Provide a "road map"—for example, a "table of contents" slide that shows a brief list of the sections of your talk.
Relying only on your voice to convey your message	Use effective visuals—diagrams, charts, maps, and photos of people—to help make your message memorable.
Presenting information-loaded visuals	Ensure that each visual conveys only one small point or piece of information.
Blocking your visuals or talking to them	Stand to the side so people can see the slides, and glance only briefly at each slide before turning to address your audience.
Using a bewildering number of visuals	Limit your visuals to only those that reinforce key points in your presentation.
Hoping that your audience will take you seriously	Inject some passion into your delivery, by reminding yourself ahead of time that you're telling them something important.
Assuming that your audience is engaged	Make eye contact with listeners and watch for fidgeting or other signs of boredom; if you see such signs, stop and ask people what's on their minds, and move in close to selected parts of your audience.
Confessing to your audience that you're nervous	Tell them how you feel about the topic you're presenting.
Grooming yourself unconsciously because you're nervous	Practice keeping your hands below your neck and above your waist.
Limiting your presentation to describing a problem	Make sure you have potential solutions to offer.
Assuming that you don't need to credit your sources	Quote sources accurately and provide proper attribution.

Sources: John Clayton, "Presentations 101: Don't Make These Common Mistakes," and "The Ten Commandments of Presentations," in *Presentations That Persuade and Motivate,* The Results-Driven Manager Series (Boston: Harvard Business School Press, 2004), 133–140, 156–163. Used with permission.

Summing Up

In this chapter, you learned that:

- The Greek approach to public speaking involves a five-part structure: introduction, narrative, argument, refutation, and conclusion. You can use the same structure for organizing and delivering business speeches and presentations.

- The introduction prepares the audience to be receptive.

- In the narrative, the speaker tells his or her story.

- In the argument, the speaker presents supporting logic.

- The speaker then uses refutation to anticipate and rebut possible objections to his or her position.

- The conclusion appeals to the audience for acceptance or a particular action.

- The four rhetorical devices used by the Greeks to connect with and convince their listeners are parallel structure, triads, antithesis, and rhetorical questions. These devices are as useful today as they were ages ago.

- The three primary learning styles of listeners are visual, auditory, and kinesthetic. Presenters should adjust their talks to the known learning style of their audiences. When the style is mixed or unknown, the speaker should include something for everyone.

- Don't simply address the intellects of your listeners; speak also to their emotions by making the personal impact of your proposal clear.

- Use a Q&A session to deepen your connection with the audience and to further persuade.

- Apply the principles of continuous process improvement to your presentation. If you do this, you will get better and better—and more persuasive—over time.

- Take steps to manage anxiety caused by fear of public speaking.

Leveraging Chapter Insights: Critical Questions

- Think of a presentation you need to give. What will you say in your speech's introduction, narrative, argument, refutation, and concluding portions?

- Recall a particularly effective presentation you heard recently. What rhetorical devices did the speaker use that you found particularly powerful? How might you work such devices into a presentation you'll be giving soon?

- How might you blend visual, auditory, and kinesthetic approaches in your presentation to better appeal to a wide range of learning styles in your audience?

- What questions do you anticipate listeners will have when you deliver your presentation? What responses to these questions can you prepare now?

- How does presentation anxiety usually manifest itself for you? What steps can you take to combat it?

- What actions might you take to continually assess the effectiveness of your presentations and make improvements?

CHAPTER NINE

The Ethics of Power, Influence, and Persuasion

Points to Honor

Key Topics Covered in This Chapter

- *Two standards to which ethical power must conform*

- *Pressures on the ethics of managers*

- *The frequent use of manipulation*

- *Ways to create an ethical culture*

P OWER, INFLUENCE, and persuasion have one thing in common with explosives. When used carefully and for well-intentioned purposes, all are capable of good. But most of us know the damage they can cause when handled carelessly, irresponsibly, or with evil or unethical intent.

Power has the capacity to corrupt those who wield it. Influence can also be malignant. And we all know of silver-tongued persuaders who will say anything, promise everything, and eventually deliver nothing. These issues, however, should not dissuade you from the legitimate uses of power, influence, and persuasion. Each has an important role to play in your ability to establish human resource programs and policies that support your company's success. This chapter addresses the ethical issues associated with their use. As we'll see, wielding your power, influence, and persuasion ethically entails more than just complying with laws and policies. Whereas compliance deals with what you *can't* do, ethics deals with what you *should* do.

The Ethical Exercise of Power

When historian Lord Acton (1832–1902) warned his students and his readers that "power tends to corrupt, and absolute power corrupts absolutely," he did so out of concern for the danger that holders of political power posed to liberty. We have seen in our own time what can happen when one person has inordinate power over others. People around the world were shocked in mid-2004 by news accounts of how some U.S. soldiers had abused and humiliated prisoners held in Iraq's Abu Ghraib jail.

Apologists cited inadequate training and lack of supervision by superior officers. But these explanations seem inadequate. At the heart of the problem was the unchecked and unaccounted-for power that the guards had over their prisoners. Oddly, the prisoner abuses exposed could have been predicted by a simulated prison experiment conducted at Stanford University in 1971 under the guidance of psychologist Philip Zimbardo. (See "The Stanford Prison Experiment" for details about this revealing study.) There, in the basement of the university's psychology department building, seemingly normal people became abusive when given power over others.

Zimbardo identified the situational settings in which atrocities such as these occur. "My research and that of my colleagues has catalogued the conditions for stirring the crucible of human nature in negative directions. Some of the necessary ingredients are: diffusion of responsibility, anonymity, dehumanization, peers who model harmful behavior, bystanders who do not intervene, and a setting of power differentials."[1] These conditions are found in some organizations.

Yes, power has the capacity to corrupt. But power is necessary to the functioning of organizations and society. How do we get constructive value from power, and not corruption and abuse? The solution is the *ethical* use of power. Power used ethically conforms to these two standards:

1. It is exercised to benefit the entity from which power is derived and that it is responsible to serve.

2. It conforms to cultural or legal standards of ethical behavior.

The first of these conditions represents the lowest order of the ethical exercise of power. Here, the person wielding power recognizes that he or she must use that power in the best interests of the organization that invested him or her with it.

For example, if an executive exercises power in support of a research project that, if successful, will benefit his organization, he is acting in an ethical manner. Thus, former General Electric CEO Jack

The Stanford Prison Experiment

The simulated prison situation set up and monitored by Zimbardo and his colleagues aimed to determine what happens when you put normal people in a situation where they have control over others—in this case, as prison guards. Would they retain their humanity, or become abusive and evil? More specifically, the team wanted to observe the psychological effects of becoming a prisoner or prison guard.

A group of mentally well-balanced, intelligent, middle-class male volunteers was randomly divided into two groups: prisoners and guards. Although both groups understood that they were merely part of a simulation, the line between simulation and reality quickly faded. As Zimbardo would write later,

> *The planned two-week study was terminated after only six days because it was out of control. Good boys chosen for their normalcy were having emotional breakdowns as powerless prisoners. Other young men chosen for their mental health and positive values eased into the character of sadistic guards inflicting suffering on their fellow students without moral compunction. And those "good guards" who did not personally debase the prisoners failed to confront the worst of their comrades, allowing evil to ripen without challenge.*

The details of the Stanford prison simulation can be viewed at http://www.prisonexp.org.

SOURCE: Philip G. Zimbardo, "Power Turns Good Soldiers into Bad Apples," *The Boston Globe,* May 9, 2004, http://www.boston.com/news/globe/editorial_opinion/oped/articles/2004/05/09/power_turns_good_soldiers_into_bad_apples.

Welch acted ethically when he used his power to obtain discretionary funds for a struggling R&D project—an unusual step outside the review process the company normally used to allocate resources. The engineers and scientists working on that project were trying to develop an X-ray system based on digital technology. Normally, project funding was conducted through a formal process, but Welch used his power of position to intervene.[2] The project eventually reached the point where it could obtain funding through normal channels, and it went on to great success, producing revenues for GE and its shareholders.

In contrast to the ethical exercise of organizational power, you can probably cite examples of people who have used the power vested in their positions for personal gain or for the benefit of their friends and family. Consider this true example:[3]

> *Dick Grasso, former chairman and CEO of the New York Stock Exchange (NYSE), resigned in September 2003 after a public outcry over a new contract he had negotiated that gave him a $140 million payout. After investigating Grasso, the NYSE turned the matter over to New York State attorney general Eliot Spitzer, who sued Grasso—demanding the return of more than $100 million.*
>
> *Grasso maintained he had a right to the full amount. But Spitzer's suit claimed that Grasso and his HR chief, Frank Ashen, had used their power to deceive and bully the exchange's board of directors into approving large increases in Grasso's compensation and allowing the CEO to circumvent accounting rules. Moreover, these abuses had roots stretching as far back as the mid-1990s.*
>
> *For example, in 1995, when Grasso wanted to claim some of his retirement funds early, a benefits consultant advised the NYSE that the transfer would require a special $12 million accounting charge. Ashen reportedly pressured the consultant not to recommend the charge, and the exchange recorded a smaller amount. The board never learned of the consultant's recommendations.*

Our second condition for the ethical exercise of power—that it must conform to cultural or legal standards of ethical behavior—trumps the first. Thus, using power to the advantage of your organization is unethical if it is illegal or if it fails to meet the standards of behavior expected by the community. Consider this example:

> *An HR consultant is empowered to represent her company's services to client companies with the goal of obtaining new business for her firm.*

If she makes the best case for those services in a truthful manner, she is acting ethically. Lying and other forms of deception might benefit her organization—at least in the short term—by generating some new business. But this behavior would violate cultural (and perhaps legal) standards of ethical behavior. In this case, she would be exercising her power unethically.

Everyone who works for an organization faces the dilemma inherent in these two aspects of ethical behavior. Here, the cynic's definition of a diplomat comes to mind: "an honest person sent abroad to lie on behalf of his country." People are routinely forced to choose between what is best for their organization and what is right in terms of higher ethical standards. Harvard professor Joseph Badaracco Jr. found clear evidence of this in a research study based principally on interviews with thirty recent Harvard Business School graduates. Badaracco describes what happened:

In many cases, [these] young managers received explicit instructions from their middle-manager bosses or felt strong organizational pressure to do things that they believed were sleazy, unethical, or sometimes illegal. Second, corporate ethics programs, codes of conduct, mission statements, hot lines, and the like provided little help. Third, many of the young managers believed that their company's executives were out-of-touch on ethical issues, either because they were too busy or because they sought to avoid responsibility.[4]

Interviewees cited pressures from their powerful bosses that put them in ethical dilemmas. One was told to make up data to support his boss's plan. "Just do it," he was told. Another cited several cases in which whistle-blowers—people who brought unethical or illegal practices to the attention of top management—met with disastrous personal consequences. Still others feared that doing the right thing would cost them their jobs.

For managers working in organizations that allow unethical behavior, the most appropriate action may be to find employment in another company—as difficult and as painful as that may be.

The Ethics of Influence and Persuasion

Whether your influence is direct or indirect, influence is most effective when it is based on mutual gain. Ethical practitioners recognize opportunities for mutual gain inherent in any situation. Indeed, this is one hallmark of a master negotiator: the ability to identify and pursue win-win opportunities. These people also consider the long-term implications of everything they do. They know that unethical tactics can destroy in an instant a reputation of trust and credibility built over years. When that reputation goes, their ability to influence goes with it.

Another violation of the ethical use of influence is manipulation. In their book *Influence Without Authority,* Allan Cohen and David Bradford define *manipulation* as "actions taken to achieve influence that would be rendered less effective if the other party knew one's actual intentions."[5] Consider these examples of unethical influence:

- **Concealing your true intentions in order to influence a better outcome for yourself.** Consider the example of a manager who is trying to rid herself of a poorly performing subordinate. "I hate to lose you," she lies, "but taking that open position in the logistics department will help you get ahead in the company."

- **Deliberately providing false information to gain advantage.** "I've heard that David Jones plans to take early retirement this year," a manager lies to an associate he is trying to recruit to his team. "So joining David's project team instead of mine would be a very bad career move for you. Once he's gone, his team will be a ship without a rudder."

"Ethical Misconduct and the Forces Behind It" provides additional examples of unethical behavior related to the abuse of influence and persuasion, as well as information about the pressures that lead to such abuses. Manipulative practices such as those just listed and those described in the box can produce short-term gains at the expense of others; these are win-lose situations. But as Cohen and Bradford point out, the manipulator is eventually found out, and his

Ethical Misconduct and the Forces Behind It

Ethical misconduct related to influence and persuasion manifests itself in numerous ways. In one survey of HR professionals, the respondents cited the following types of misconduct they had seen in their organizations (figures in parentheses indicate the rates at which those forms were observed):

- Management lying to employees, customers, vendors, or the public (31 percent)

- Lying on reports and falsifying records (28 percent)

- Withholding needed information from employees, customers, vendors, or the public (18 percent)

- Violating employees' privacy (16 percent)

- Accepting or giving bribes, kickbacks, or inappropriate gifts (14 percent)

- Obtaining competitors' proprietary information (8 percent)

- Altering results of product or service testing (7 percent)

- Misuse of organization's proprietary information (6 percent)

- Misrepresenting company's financial assets (5 percent)

- Misusing insider information (3 percent)

- Management lying to shareholders (2 percent)

- Withholding information from shareholders (2 percent)

Clearly, lying and withholding information count among the most frequent forms of ethical misconduct related to influence and persuasion—though violating privacy and accepting or giving bribes, kickbacks, or inappropriate gifts also occur quite often compared with other types of misconduct. What explains the frequency of these forms of misconduct? According to this same study, people who compromise their organization's ethics standards do so because they feel various forms of pressure. These include the following:

- An attempt to meet overly aggressive business or financial objectives (50 percent)

- The perceived need to follow a boss's directives (49 percent)

- Desire to meet schedule pressures (38 percent)

- Desire to help the organization survive (30 percent)

- Rationalization that "others do it" (22 percent)

- Resistance to competitive threats (18 percent)

- Attempt to advance a boss's career interests (15 percent)

- Peer pressure (12 percent)

SOURCE: Joshua Joseph and Evren Esen, *2003 Business Ethics Survey* (Alexandria, VA: Society for Human Resource Management, 2003), 6, 8. Used with permission.

or her future ability to influence is compromised, making that individual ineffective in future dealings. "Fooling some of the people some of the time is not enough for sustained success in today's interdependent organizations," they write. "Those who lie to get their way are almost inevitably found out and then frozen out of the action by peers and bosses who do not trust them ... A reputation for shady practices, or even for constant self-interest at the expense of others, is corrosive; colleagues and bosses resist the influence attempts of those they don't trust."[6]

A Solution

Power, influence, and persuasion are necessary as well as dangerous, and they create ethical dilemmas. Some people must have greater power than others in order to influence behavior and make tough decisions. But that same power can be used in malicious ways. People must also apply persuasion in order to get things done, but powers of persuasion are always only a step away from self-serving manipulation.

The major scandals that have scourged the business world in recent years have caused a fundamental change in the way the public perceives corporations. This shift places a new burden on HR practitioners and other executives to push for ethical performance by leaders not only in their personal actions but also in the company's policies and practices. In short, there's a growing belief that corporations and their leaders can and should be held accountable for their actions.[7]

Can anything be done to neutralize or eliminate the ethical dilemmas associated with power, influence, and persuasion? The answer is yes. Top management and corporate boards can reduce or eliminate them by doing the following:

- Aligning company policies and standards with the highest legal and ethical expectations of behavior.

- Vigorously enforcing those policies and standards.

- Including ethical performance in appraisals of individual job performance—and taking it seriously.

- Seeing to it that executives and managers who are invested with power are morally and ethically equipped to use it wisely.

- Serving as visible models of ethical behavior by acting wisely and temperately in their use of power, influence, and persuasion. Senior managers can be models of ethical behavior only if they get out of their offices and interact with people at lower levels.

Given the troubling number of ethical problems in the business world today, HR practitioners can—and should—take responsibility for ensuring that individuals throughout their organizations strive for the highest possible ethical behavior. By "owning" this issue, HR professionals demonstrate their value as strategic partners in their enterprise. Indeed, 43 percent of respondents in one survey of HR professionals agreed that the HR department is a "primary ethics resource" in their organization—meaning that the department develops ethics communications, provides training in ethics standards, handles ethics inquiries and reports, and offers additional ethics-related services.[8] In this same study, 44 percent of the respondents agreed that HR professionals in their organizations are also involved in formulating ethics policies.[9]

How can HR practitioners have the best possible impact on efforts to ensure ethical behavior in the use of power, influence, and persuasion? They can apply each of the practices listed previously. In addition, they can take the following steps:

- **Craft a formal code of ethics.** Work with your organization's general counsel to create an ethics code that includes standards related to power, influence, and persuasion.

- **Communicate the code.** Make sure prospective employees, new hires, and long-standing employees understand your company's code of ethics. Formally communicate the code on a regular basis (many companies do so annually), and have employees recertify that they are in compliance with it.

- **Follow the code of ethics meticulously yourself.** By modeling ethical behavior and adherence to the code, you inspire similar behavior in others.

- **Provide ethics training.** Design and deliver ethics training sessions featuring realistic case studies and open discussion of ethics issues.

- **Clarify the process for reporting ethics violations.** To enable compliance with the ethics standards your company has defined, provide an ethics hotline or an ombudsperson whereby employees can get answers to questions and concerns about ethics issues without fear of punishment. Identify someone as the person to call if an employee is reporting a breach of ethics or needs help deciding whether such a breach has occurred.

- **Make it clear that all employees—including those at the highest levels—are required to follow the code.** Point out that anyone who violates the code of ethics will be subject to penalties, regardless of his or her position in the organization.

- **Support your company's ethics office.**[10] Some companies establish an ethics office within the HR function, whereas others create two separate entities. If the latter situation describes your organization, you can support the ethics office in numerous ways. For example, suggest that high-potential executives rotate through ethics positions to round out their corporate experience. The benefit? Eventually, your company's senior management ranks will be populated by people who have spent time in the ethics office and learned the importance of ethics compliance for the organization's bottom line.

These activities may seem like idealistic solutions, but they easily fall within the capacity of HR professionals, other senior managers, and the directors to whom they ultimately report. Together, you and they can create a culture of ethical behavior that is self-policing and self-perpetuating and that sets a high standard for all employees.

Power, influence, and persuasion can be used for both good and evil. The challenge for management is to create an organizational culture in which the good side prevails.

Summing Up

In this chapter, you learned that:

- Power used ethically conforms to each of the following standards: it is exercised to benefit the entity from which power is derived and that it is responsible to serve, and it conforms to cultural or legal standards of ethical behavior. The second of these standards trumps the first.

- Ethical influence and persuasion are most effective when based on mutual gain.

- Manipulation is the greatest ethical danger in the exercise of influence.

- HR professionals, other senior managers, and directors can reduce or eliminate ethical problems if they (1) align company policies and standards with the highest legal and ethical expectations of behavior, (2) enforce those policies and standards, (3) include ethical performance in appraisals of job performance, (4) make certain that people given power have the moral and ethical capacity to use it wisely, and (5) act as models of ethical behavior. Additional steps include establishing and communicating a code of ethics that covers abuses related to power, influence, and persuasion, as well as providing ongoing training on ethics.

Leveraging Chapter Insights: Critical Questions

- What, if any, types of ethical misconduct related to the abuse of power, influence, and persuasion have you seen in your organization?

- In your view, what kinds of pressures may be leading to these abuses?

- What steps might you take to reduce the pressures that lead to such abuses?

- Does your organization have an ethics function (including an ethics officer)? If so, where is that function located? (Within HR? As a separate entity?) If the ethics function is separate from HR, how might you strengthen HR's support of the function?

- Does your company have a code of ethics? If so, does the code prohibit clearly defined ethical misconduct related to power, influence, and persuasion? If not, how might you ensure that such language is incorporated into the code?

CHAPTER TEN

Becoming an HR Star

Lessons in Power, Influence,
and Persuasion

Key Topics Covered in This Chapter

- *Starting your new role on the right foot*

- *Forging positive relationships with higher-ups*

- *Getting your staff on board*

- *Collaborating with peers*

- *Winning buy-in for HR initiatives*

- *Wielding your power, influence, and persuasion skills during tough times*

- *Avoiding abuse of HR's power*

A S AN H R professional, you routinely face numerous situations in which your savvy use of power, influence, and persuasion can make or break your effectiveness as a leader. Winning buy-in for HR initiatives and rallying others during difficult times are just two examples. You also must interact with a wide variety of key constituencies to gain support and cooperation for your ideas. These constituencies include "higher-ups" (such as your CEO and other top executives in the company), your staff, and peer managers and executives.

Moreover, your timing in exercising power, influence, and persuasion matters. For instance, if you're new to the HR managerial role, the way you comport yourself and build networks of influence in the initial days of your job can strongly determine your effectiveness later. Finally, no matter how seasoned a leader you are, you must always guard against abuse of HR's power. In this age of increasing competition in the business arena, the temptation to misuse power is all too widespread.

This chapter explores each of these dimensions of power, influence, and persuasion, using case studies of HR executives who have applied these important skills effectively in a variety of contexts—as well as some who have exercised these skills unethically. By drawing lessons from these executives' stories, you can identify potent ways of using your own power, influence, and persuasion skills. Let's now take a closer look at the many different contexts in which you employ these skills, and meet some of the HR practitioners who have valuable lessons to share.

Starting Your New Role on the Right Foot

Whether you're just starting out in your career as an HR manager or you've recently gotten a job as an HR leader in a new company, you need to carefully lay the groundwork for using your power and exercising your influence and persuasion skills. Otherwise, you'll stand little chance of enacting the changes needed to help your company improve its performance. Establishing credibility and knowing how to diplomatically mold your organization's culture can help you set the stage for exercising these skills. Ensuring that the HR function serves as a business partner is also essential.

The following story reveals how one successful HR executive started her new role on the right foot:[1]

In 1996, Bedford, Massachusetts–based defense contractor MITRE Corporation divested part of its operation. The company's executive team then hired Lisa Bender as HR director, charging her with professionalizing and modernizing the company, as well as enabling HR to work as an integrated team rather than a "stovepipe."

Bender had no formal HR training. But thanks to her background in organizational development and her degree in social psychology, she possessed the ability to exercise crucial HR skills, such as diagnosing problems quickly, seeing the big picture, communicating well with others, and winning others' support for changes. Her biggest challenge as she started in her new role? Deciding how best to work with a very formal organizational culture dominated by male engineers who, by their own admission, felt uncomfortable with "people issues." MITRE's engineering experts were "very smart," said Bender. And, "as experts in their own fields, they [expected] to be experts in everything else, including HR."

Bender quickly decided that her most important task was to establish her credibility with MITRE's workforce. She set out to show the engineers that she knew what she was doing—by talking with them about their business and asking them what they were trying to accomplish. Through these moves, she defied their expectation that she would "just do as she was told" rather than asking probing questions.

Bender also set out to position HR as a business partner throughout MITRE. Specifically, she established a team of HR professionals,

Lessons for Starting Out on the Right Foot

- **Do** take stock of the organizational culture that characterizes your organization. Develop strategies for molding the culture to enable execution of important HR initiatives.

- **Don't** fulfill inappropriate expectations of your role held by the workforce. For example, if people expect you not to ask questions, experiment with defying that assumption.

- **Do** move early to establish your credibility in the minds of superiors, peers, and direct reports. To build credibility, demonstrate your skills and knowledge, and show genuine interest in key constituencies' work.

- **Don't** assume that HR's job is to fulfill requests from the company's various units. Instead, create structures and establish processes that enable HR to serve as a business partner to the units.

- **Do** seek ways to support your company's CEO, whether it's providing impromptu coaching, helping him or her build a convincing business case for an important initiative, or generating ideas for addressing thorny business challenges.

- **Do** treat your company's employees as professionals when introducing new HR programs. For instance, enabling people to determine how they use leave time encourages a sense of responsibility and ownership and can help improve morale and job satisfaction.

headed by a manager, for each of the company's six business units. Each team handles its unit's day-to-day HR needs. Unit managers have embraced the new model because it enables them to go to one person with HR questions and concerns. The HR-as-business-partner model also helps Bender do her job better. When she meets with HR man-

*agers, she gains important information and insights into business trends
and each unit's specific current needs. Armed with this knowledge, she
can push for new initiatives during meetings with company officers.*

*As another smart initial move, Bender looked for opportunities
to support her CEO. To illustrate, when he mentioned an incident
in which he had failed to persuade someone to see his viewpoint, she
suggested an alternative way of presenting his case. He tried her suggestion, and it worked. He expressed his appreciation with a heartfelt
"Thanks, Coach!"*

*Owing to her savvy early efforts, Bender succeeded in implement-
ing major HR changes. For example, she introduced a new flextime
policy, a performance management program, and a plan for paying
employees for unused leave time—all of which won wide approval.
Her new programs attracted attention from external observers as well:
MITRE became one of only seven U.S. companies to make* Fortune
*magazine's list of the one hundred best companies to work for—for
three years running. In addition, in 2001, Bender was promoted to vice
president and chief human resources officer of the company at the
recommendation of the CEO.*

For a summary of the lessons offered by Bender's experience, see
"Lessons for Starting Out on the Right Foot."

Forging Positive Relationships with Higher-Ups

To launch valuable new HR programs or make changes to existing
policies and initiatives, you need to forge positive relationships with
the higher-ups in your organization—your boss in HR, the CEO,
and the board of directors. By establishing your credibility, linking
proposed programs to higher-ups' priorities, and cultivating mutual
trust in these relationships, you boost your chances of successfully
wielding your power, influence, and persuasion skills—especially in
situations where a higher-up rejects your proposal or you need to
raise sensitive concerns about his or her policies or behavior. The
following anecdote offers important lessons for all HR executives:[2]

HR manager Lynda Ford vastly strengthened her influence with her organization's CEO by keying in on his goals and priorities for the business and adapting her choice of language to his preferred style. She had an opportunity to wield these skills when she proposed that recruiters interview prospective employees for specific jobs at each of the firm's forty sites, rather than conducting the interviews at headquarters. Her reasoning? With the current system, "hires went to whichever manager was squawking the loudest. But each site had its own culture and environment, and not everybody was a good fit." As a result, turnover rose.

But when Ford pitched her idea to the CEO, he turned it down— arguing that he didn't understand why the company had to "waste time" by having recruiters work out of the office. His perception, according to Ford, was that "if you're not strapped to your desk in corporate, you're not being productive."

To persuade the CEO to reconsider her idea, Ford latched on to his buzzwords: "wasting time." "To him," she realized, "wasting time meant money out the window." So she compared the cost of making a bad hire with the cost of getting recruiters out of headquarters. Her analysis revealed that the company would get a huge return on its investment by changing the recruiting process as she described. Impressed by the numbers, the CEO agreed to try Ford's idea.

Everyone benefited. The company's list of open positions dropped from just over seventy to sixteen in less than a month, and the time needed to fill vacancies decreased—a critical step in controlling overtime. Moreover, because HR was more effectively assessing candidates' "fit" with unit culture, turnover decreased. Equally important, Ford began building a track record of success—which further enhanced her credibility with the CEO.

Ford's early successes enabled her to drive larger change in her organization later. For instance, she ultimately persuaded the CEO to support a Total Quality Management (TQM) initiative at the company by bringing another executive on board who championed TQM. Hearing the benefits that this executive gained, in addition to considering Ford's analysis of the potential benefits, helped convince top man-

agement to commit to TQM. Indeed, four years later, the organization received a state award for excellence in quality processes.

For a closer look at the lessons in Ford's story, as well as additional strategies for building positive relationships with your boss and other senior executives, see "Lessons for Forging Productive Relationships with Higher Ups."

Lessons for Forging Productive Relationships with Higher-Ups

- **Do** bring only the most important issues—those affecting the company's ability to execute its strategy—to higher-ups.

- **Don't** forget to assess your boss's and other key senior executives' preferences even before you're hired or before a new senior leader starts at your company. For example, ask how your soon-to-be chief executive would like you to address a sensitive subject or difference of opinion. Pick up on verbal and nonverbal cues that reveal his or her receptivity to your ideas.

- **Do** identify higher-ups' hot buttons—such as sensitivity to certain terms—and identify ways to avoid pressing those buttons.

- **Don't** assume that you know what your CEO's goals and priorities for the business are. Ask him or her, and then link your proposals to achievement of those goals. You'll stand a better chance of getting a fair hearing for your ideas.

- **Do** find out higher-ups' communication preferences. Does your boss or CEO want detailed reports or short summaries? Does he or she prefer you to present challenges on paper or in person?

continued

- **Don't** go barging into a higher-up's office to present an idea without practicing your presentation first. Ask a trusted colleague to listen to your presentation first and evaluate whether your argument hangs together logically. That person can also pose worst-case-scenario questions for you.

- **Do** get your facts and figures straight. Have all the information supporting your case at your fingertips, and provide copies to your audience so he or she can review the information later.

- **Don't** present ideas or challenges to higher-ups in an emotionally charged manner. Instead of making "you" statements, use "I" or "we" statements so you don't come across as pointing fingers.

- **Do** follow up a successful pitch to a higher-up with a memo outlining what you've agreed to and which steps need to be taken next. If the senior executive asks you to gather more information on your idea, find out when he or she expects it, or estimate how long it will take you to provide it. Then stick to that commitment.

- **Don't** take it personally if a higher-up rejects your idea. Instead, acknowledge the opposing stand, study the reasoning behind it, and consider ways to counter resistance with compelling facts and figures.

The Board of Directors

Your boss and the CEO are just a few of the higher-ups you need to influence. Nowadays, many HR professionals are also interacting more frequently with the board of directors' compensation committee.[3] Why? The Sarbanes-Oxley Act of 2002 presented board compensation committees with new regulations and increasingly complex financial reporting requirements intended to protect shareholders' investments.

The act contains sweeping legislation affecting corporate governance, disclosure, and financial accounting at public companies. In addition, it stipulates new laws regarding executive compensation—for example, it prevents company loans to executives and directors and stiffens penalties for violations of the Employee Retirement Income Security Act (ERISA).

What does all this mean for HR? Most board compensation committees find it exceedingly difficult to stay on top of complex compensation matters. Thus, they rely on outside consultants to provide objective analysis. But they need HR to determine whether the consultants' recommendations align with organizational goals. For that reason, many committees are looking to HR to give their impressions of consultants' suggestions and articulate the corporation's compensation philosophy.

You can strongly influence the compensation committee by reviewing consultants' recommendations with committee members and helping them understand why specific advice has been offered. Engage them in dialogue about alternatives as well. Drawing on your knowledge of how the organization operates, give the committee your impressions about whether the recommendations make sense, and identify any flaws or inconsistencies that you spot in the consultants' suggestions.

You'll need the confidence to push back when you see management doing something that doesn't seem right. In a businesslike way, tell board members how shareholders might view a particular action. Be sure to speak up if what you see happening doesn't strike you as proper governance.

You can further strengthen your influence with the board by providing thorough competitive data about what other companies are doing regarding compensation and how your organization's practices compare with others in the same industry. But also know when to focus on your company's unique needs rather than others' practices. The real skill lies in understanding when it's time to emulate others and when it's time to develop practices best suited for *your* organization.

Getting Your Staff on Board

To get your staff on board—that is, to influence them to perform at their best and embrace needed changes—you can't rely solely on your formal authority over them. To be sure, bossing people (for example, threatening to fire them if they don't follow orders) may get you some degree of compliance in the short run. But it won't get you *commitment*—the heartfelt desire to excel and support your company's mission over the long haul.

To win your staff's commitment, not force their compliance, you need to exert your influence and hone your persuasion skills. That gets easier when you treat your people with respect and fairness, clarify what you expect of them, help them develop their skills, listen carefully to their concerns, and recognize and reward constructive behavior. The following anecdote shows how one HR professional applied these practices:[4]

> *Siobhan Callahan was the HR director at a large corporation. Victor Brown, a supervisor in her department, wanted to be promoted to a managerial position. But Siobhan didn't believe that Victor had developed his skills enough to be effective as a manager. She told him she had decided against promoting him. When Victor expressed strong disappointment and asked for an explanation, Siobhan listened with empathy to his concerns. She reflected the emotions she was hearing, and she invited Victor to talk about his career ambitions. She remained attentive and relaxed, and maintained eye contact during the conversation.*
>
> *Siobhan might have been tempted to sugarcoat her explanation for why she wasn't promoting Victor—for example, attributing her decision to budget constraints. But instead, she calmly and honestly explained her reasoning, including the factors she took into account in making her decision. For instance, she listed specific skills needed in the managerial role and described in concrete terms the skill areas Victor would need to develop in order to qualify.*
>
> *She also coached Victor. She reassured him that she was interested in his success, and described in precise terms what he needed to do to improve his chances at a later promotion. She then encouraged him to*

sign up for training opportunities and other resources that she believed would help him. During the conversation, she invited Victor to have a say in the goals and targets they defined—knowing that people feel more committed to outcomes when they've had a voice in defining them and generating ideas for achieving them.

In the months following this conversation, Siobhan met regularly with Victor to assess his progress. She recognized his successes with genuine expressions of appreciation. And she offered him special assignments in which he had expressed interest and which would help him strengthen the skills he needed in order to become a manager. After a year and a half, she was delighted to award Victor the promotion.

Siobhan's treatment of Victor, and the results that her managerial style generated, have much to teach all leaders who are seeking to influence and motivate their staff to perform at their best. For a summary of the key points in Siobhan's story, as well as additional tips, see "Lessons for Getting Your Staff on Board."

Lessons for Getting Your Staff on Board

- **Do** practice empathetic listening when a staff member expresses concern or frustration over a decision you've made or a change you've initiated.

- **Don't** sugarcoat disappointing news or lie about the reasons behind an unpopular decision. You'll only earn the distrust of your staff once they discover the truth—as they inevitably will do.

- **Do** express your expectations—and the consequences for failing to meet those expectations—in ways that respect your employees' dignity.

- **Don't** assume that your staff members will know what's needed to succeed. Help them clarify the skills they must

continued

develop to support the company's goals and further their own career ambitions.

- **Do** confront less-than-optimal behavior in a private, professional way. Express concern in terms of behavior and its impact on your team and the company—not in terms of character judgments or assumptions about the person's motives.

- **Don't** leave it up to your people to tell you their career aspirations. Regularly meet to discuss their goals and the ways in which you can help them achieve their objectives and tie their professional achievements to your company's needs.

- **Do** seek other managers' perspectives on major decisions, when appropriate. Pay extra attention to colleagues who have a different interpretation of the situation at hand than you do. They'll help you keep an open mind.

- **Don't** impose decisions or changes in policies on your people without getting their input. Before committing to rules or procedures that affect them, people need to feel that they've had a voice in the matter.

- **Do** be open to an employee's decision to seek an impartial review of an unpopular decision you've made. Your people have the right to such a review without being made to feel guilty or subversive.

- **Don't** hesitate to acknowledge when you've made a mistake or used inaccurate information in making a decision regarding an employee or introducing a change to a policy or procedure.

SOURCES: Kelly Mollica, "Perceptions of Fairness," *HR Magazine,* June 2004; Robert N. Llewellyn, "The Power in Being a People Developer," *HR Magazine,* July 2002; R. Brayton Bowen, "Practice the Five R's to Motivate Workers," SHRM white paper, Society for Human Resource Management, Alexandria, VA; Jathan W. Janove, "Speak Softly and Carry a Big Stick," *HR Magazine,* January 2003; and Madelyn Burley-Allen, "Listen Up," *HR Magazine,* November 2001. Used with permission.

Collaborating with Peers

The quality of your collaboration with peer managers and executives can strongly shape your ability to exercise your power, influence, and persuasion in your organization. Of course, your most important collaborative relationship is with the CEO. However, the way in which you interact with other leaders also plays a crucial role in your effectiveness.

For example, some experts maintain that an effective relationship between a company's HR executive and its chief information officer (CIO) is critical to the success of HR strategies. Why? Much of an HR executive's success hinges on technology-enabled HR processes (such as employee self-service). To get results that will satisfy the CEO, the HR executive and CIO must have a strong partnership and collaborate in an atmosphere of mutual trust and respect.

Yet trust and respect between HR and CIO leaders remain elusive at many companies, owing to persistent stereotypes. For instance, some IT experts assume that HR professionals aren't clear, analytical thinkers. For their part, some HR practitioners view IT professionals as lacking interpersonal skills and unable to appreciate the human side of business.

How can you combat these stereotypes and cultivate a positive relationship with your company's CIO? The following true story offers important lessons:[5]

> Mike Williams, senior vice president of HR, and Greg Wilson, CIO, both work at power company TransAlta Group in Calgary. The two men have strived to cultivate a productive partnership specifically to realize their common vision: helping their organization become more effective and productive. Williams tackles this effort from "a people point of view," while Wilson does so through process and technology.
>
> The two executives have used numerous strategies to build a strong relationship. For example, from the beginning of their employment at TransAlta, they each tried to learn "who's who" at the company and what the organization's most pressing issues were. These efforts spawned conversations between them, during which they each realized

that a productive relationship would be essential to one another's ability to score successes on the job.

Williams and Wilson have also drawn on similarities in their backgrounds to forge a partnership. For instance, both had accumulated management experience outside of HR and IT in previous positions. The broad business knowledge they gained from this experience has enabled them to understand sweeping technological trends and their implications for TransAlta. In addition, the two men share the belief that "salesmanship"—persuading the workforce to back major HR and IT initiatives—is a big part of their jobs.

To continually strengthen their working relationship, Williams and Wilson meet formally once a month and participate in executive-team meetings every other week. They also talk informally as neces-sary to maintain a continuous dialogue on the initiatives they're driving.

Their efforts have paid big dividends. To illustrate, the two execu-tives have made huge improvements in TransAlta's use of SAP, a technology platform that enables employee self-service and other pro-cess improvements. When Williams and Wilson first started at the company, the SAP platform was collecting data. However, aside from the corporate and financial centers and the HR staff, people throughout the company weren't widely using the SAP applications. "There was a superficial understanding of technology, and an environment in which employees expected things to be done for them," noted Wil-liams. "The challenge was how to get the organization to embrace [SAP]."

Drawing on their previous experience at high-tech firms in which business processes had been automated, Williams and Wilson worked together to encourage broader use of SAP throughout the company. Thanks to their ability to collaborate effectively, they succeeded: automa-tion allowed the firm to reduce its HR staff to thirty-five from fifty-four. And Williams estimated that HR-related technology had a return on investment of 107 percent in 2003 alone.

For a distillation of lessons from these two leaders' story, see "Lessons for Collaborating with Peers."

Lessons for Collaborating with Peers

- **Do** clarify a shared vision and goals with the peer executives whose collaboration you need to carry out important HR initiatives.

- **Don't** rely only on happenstance encounters to engage in conversations with key peers. Set up regular meetings with them and other executives to discuss major issues and initiatives. Attend meetings led by peer executives so as to represent HR concerns and help build bridges across functions in the company. Such meetings give participants from different functions a new understanding of one another's challenges.

- **Do** brainstorm strategies for selling important initiatives (whether in HR or other functions) to the rest of your company.

- **Don't** assume that HR experience is the be-all and end-all in collaborating effectively with peers. Many experts believe that the best HR practitioners today are businesspeople first—that is, they have a broad range of experience as well as extensive profit-and-loss responsibility.

- **Do** work with your peers to develop a compelling business case for each new initiative you propose.

- **Don't** underestimate the power of physical proximity to peer executives. By locating your office close to those of key peers, you make it easier to engage in frequent ad hoc exchanges of ideas.

Winning Buy-in for Strategic HR Initiatives

HR practitioners have a vital role to play in enabling their organizations to carry out their competitive strategy. People have become the most important asset for knowledge companies, so HR management practices constitute crucial components in any corporation's strategy. Indeed, firms with the most HR practices that reinforce top-notch performance tend to have the highest market value per employee. To develop and win support for strategic HR initiatives—those that help your company achieve its mission and remain competitive— you need to make (and sell) savvy decisions about HR's structure, your function's links to its internal customers, competency development, management processes, rewards, and use of IT, to name a few. Smart choices and good communication about these matters can help you further deploy scarce resources to deliver strategic value to your company.

How can you make strategic choices that will earn the backing of other leaders in your company? Apportion the majority of your time to optimizing the performance of your organization's workforce so that they can boost the company's performance overall. That means understanding how your business works, which processes are working well and which aren't, and what the organization's goals are—as well as being able to put plans in place to achieve those goals. Developing a broad range of experience and collaborating productively with other executives throughout your company are additional important keys to delivering strategic value through HR.

Consider this HR professional's story:[6]

Kathleen Barclay is vice president of global human resources at General Motors. Her previous management positions, including profit-and-loss responsibility, have helped her develop strong business acumen. Thanks to her broad background, she has a clear understanding of what GM needs to do to be successful—and how HR can contribute to that success. She also doesn't hesitate to leverage the creative power of other executives and peers throughout her organization. Thanks to these skills, she has been able to implement important initiatives designed to tackle GM's thorniest challenges.

For example, to stem the rising tide of health-care costs, Barclay has developed "an inclusive strategy that combines creative ideas from all parts of the business, whether it's our financial partners, technology partners, people in human resources, government relations, quality, manufacturing, and beyond . . . It is truly a multifunctional team that comes together." Owing to the collaborative brainstorming and idea execution Barclay has facilitated, GM has found ways to control cost increases more than its competitors have.

Barclay has also successfully molded GM's culture to emphasize speed and agility—essential characteristics in the automotive industry. The company's "GoFast" initiative has led to the elimination of unproductive meetings, removed layers of corporate bureaucracy, accelerated decision making, and energized employees. Leaders at GM feel convinced that GoFast has helped raise the company's "direct-run rate"—a metric related to vehicles produced without glitches.

To generate additional valuable ideas, Barclay also participates in high-level strategy discussions. For instance, before GM acquired Korean automaker Daewoo, she helped company leaders think through questions such as "Who will staff key positions?" "What kind of cultural approach are we going to put in the business plan?" and "What's the organizational structure [of the new entity] going to look like?" Such conversations generate insights that help Barclay determine how her HR team can best move the business forward. In other words: "What are the most important business levers that are people-related, whether it's increasing the volume on this particular product or it's a labor negotiation relative to wage rate?"

"Lessons for Winning Buy-in for Strategic HR Initiatives" sums up the lessons in Barclay's story and offers additional recommendations.

Lessons for Winning Buy-in for Strategic HR Initiatives

- **Do** invest most of your time and mental energy to thinking about ways to help your company boost its performance.

- **Don't** take on roles limited to HR: build broad business experience both within a particular company and among different companies.

continued

- **Do** constantly take the pulse of your organization—asking what's working well and what isn't, and how HR can help the company reach its goals.

- **Don't** make aggressive demands for resources or new organizational structures for HR. Build your credibility first, and demonstrate that you can add value through strategic HR initiatives.

- **Do** persuade your company to invest in a high-quality HR information system to increase HR's credibility and the perception of value it adds, while decreasing the time your function spends on administrative tasks.

- **Don't** force HR services on division leaders. Instead, give them the opportunity to find better deals if they can. This will help create an open-market atmosphere, prompting HR to deliver economically useful services.

- **Do** provide copious data to business leaders throughout your organization on how they're performing (against human capital benchmarks) relative to one another and external competitors.

- **Don't** let performance data just pile up; interpret those numbers and apply their lessons to extend best practices throughout your organization.

- **Do** demonstrate in concrete terms the bottom-line impact of strategic HR initiatives.

Wielding Power, Influence, and Persuasion During Tough Times

Exercising your power, influence, and persuasion skillfully becomes even more important during tough times—whether those times involve turning around a failing company, helping your organization recover from a natural disaster or terrorist attack, or addressing destructive political infighting. During such times, you'll need focus, determination, strong communication skills, and clarity about your company's goals in order to generate value for your company and win buy-in for your HR initiatives. The following anecdote reveals how one HR professional accomplished all of this:[7]

> *Patricia Nazemetz, vice president of human resources for Xerox Corporation, faced a major challenge in 2000. The company needed to engineer a turnaround—quickly. It was $17.1 billion in debt, its stock had plummeted, and it had suffered seven straight losing quarters. The CEO had initiated a large-scale cost-cutting effort, which included drastically downsizing the workforce and stopping all internal training and other HR programs deemed nonessential. At the same time, Xerox needed to prevent its best talent from flocking to the exits.*
>
> *Nazemetz and her staff had to persuade the company's most valuable employees to decide against deserting what many people viewed as a sinking ship. They quickly formulated potent retention strategies. For example, they sent a strong message of caring to employees through town meetings and media such as audio, video, and print. The CEO personalized the message by traveling "around the world three times within two months delivering the 'We can't survive without you' message."*
>
> *Company leaders set a target of 95 percent retention of high-potential employees. To achieve that target, the HR group took steps to ensure that the valued individuals received "the right experiences, job assignments, visibility, and learning opportunities . . . to prepare them for executive leadership positions."*
>
> *A newly appointed chief talent officer established "a virtual consulting business within the company, traversing the nation and the globe to make sure those high performers got the right personal touch and understood their roles in the company's transformation." Another key HR move consisted of "strategy alignment workshops"—"get-togethers facilitated by HR so everyone is on the same page relative to the 'new' Xerox." At these workshops, Nazemetz explains, "People talk about what's going to get in the way of us achieving success . . . what is missing, what resonates, and how to remove any roadblocks."*

These efforts paid off. In just the first twelve months of the turn-around, Xerox kept more than 97 percent of the high-value employees it had targeted for retention—beating its goal of 95 percent. In 2003, the company's net income more than tripled, and its stock price recovered to impressive levels. Company leaders felt hopeful about eliminating debt entirely, and "analysts from major brokerage houses . . . recommended Xerox as a 'buy.'"

Nazemetz's story contains valuable lessons for other HR experts. See "Lessons for Exercising Power, Influence, and Persuasion During Tough Times" for a summary of these lessons, as well as additional tips.

Lessons for Exercising Power, Influence, and Persuasion During Tough Times

- **Do** remain focused on your company's highest-level objectives during tough times, while also developing strategies for influencing key constituents.

- **Don't** shrink from making the painful decisions needed to enable your company to survive a crisis or downturn—whether those decisions involve cutting "luxury" initiatives, severely downsizing your organization's workforce, or defining some other difficult choice.

- **Do** use every possible communication channel—face-to-face presentations, e-mail, print, and so forth—to convey the message people need to hear in order to usher your company through its difficulty.

- **Don't** assume that only money will motivate people to rally around a troubled organization. People are also powerfully moved by genuine expressions of appreciation of the value that they bring to the table.

- **Do** help company leaders to establish clear metrics for success during difficult times, such as "retaining our best people." Ensure that each metric has a clear target, such as "95 percent retention of identified high performers."

- **Don't** focus only on short-term goals. Identify long-term changes—such as improving leadership bench strength at three levels for each position, or reducing turnover 20 percent over the next five years—that you'll need to enact in order to help your company recover from the difficult period.

- **Do** ensure that employees' emotional needs are met during hard times—whether it's their need to feel valued during a drastic downsizing or their need to know who to call or where to go for crucial information during an emergency.

- **Don't** underestimate the power of contingency planning. When times are good, develop systems and structures (such as back-up offices or information systems) that you know your company will need during a crisis.

- **Do** brace yourself to go above and beyond the call of duty during difficult times. Especially during crises, you and your staff may need to work around the clock to ensure that your company's human capital is safe and able to return to their normal responsibilities as quickly as possible.

Avoiding the Abuse of HR's Power

Like other executives, high-level HR professionals possess substantial power and influence.[8] They can play a major role in decisions about which vendors the company will use, who will get hired for key positions in the company, and which initiatives are implemented in their organization. They also have access to confidential information—for example, financial data about their company and personal information about each of its employees. For individuals who have few scruples and a keen desire to further their own interests, this degree of power and influence can prove all too tempting to abuse.

Some experts maintain that ethical lapses among HR leaders are particularly damaging to an organization—perhaps because many people look to HR to embody and communicate their company's values and shape a culture characterized by honesty and integrity. When workers learn that HR executives whom they trusted and in whom they placed their confidence have benefited themselves at the corporation's expense, morale and productivity plummet.

Fraudulent conduct, in particular, has shown disturbing trends in recent years. For example, a whopping 75 percent of respondents in one 2003 survey said they had experienced fraud in their organizations—up from 62 percent in 1998. Another survey found that one of every four employee crimes was committed by an executive, and more than half are committed by management.

Consider the following story of one HR leader who was accused of abusing his power through fraudulent conduct:[9]

Hired as America Online's executive vice president of HR in November 2002 at just thirty-six years of age, Gregory Horton boasted a resume studded with plum HR positions at star companies such as PepsiCo and Qwest Communications. Yet within less than a year, AOL had fired Horton. It then filed suit against him (still pending), charging him with fraud, business conspiracy, and other alleged malfeasance. The lawsuit seeks damages for "coercing AOL and its contractors to enter in sham contracts, and then improperly diverting the contract payments" to a "sham corporation" allegedly owned by Horton and others named in the suit.

AOL had carefully checked Horton's background and references, and it asked him to sign a corporate standards-of-business-conduct document it had developed. It was the internal auditing procedures established after an SEC probe of AOL's reporting of advertising revenues that quickly exposed questionable behaviors.

The company's internal auditors spotted a $100,000 contract for consulting services related to an employee survey instrument, signed by Horton and the owner of a consulting company. The auditors noted that the contract's scope of work included a planning session with Horton and Linda Simon, who was in charge of the survey instrument. When *the auditors asked Simon about the planning session, she knew nothing about it. She called the consulting firm to ask what was going on, and was told, "Don't worry about it." That's when the red flag went up.*

The suit alleges that the $100,000 went through the consulting company to several other firms owned by Horton and other former colleagues from his PepsiCo days. AOL is accusing Horton and these colleagues of having an agreement to engage in fraudulent conduct even before Horton joined AOL.

AOL's unfortunate experience suggests the need for companies to take firm steps to prevent abuse of HR's power. "Lessons for Avoiding the Abuse of HR's Power" offers recommendations.

Lessons for Avoiding the Abuse of HR's Power

- **Do** follow the highest level of ethics yourself.

- **Do** use unethical incidents involving HR as teaching opportunities—by taking immediate and appropriate action to demonstrate your organization's standards.

- **Don't** walk on eggshells when you see signs of unethical or illegal practices by HR professionals in your organization. If something strikes you as wrong, follow up on it to determine the details.

- **Do** reinforce written standards of business conduct with clear messages from top leaders—including yourself—that such standards are more than words on a page. Issue strong statements that unethical behavior won't be tolerated.

- **Don't** forget to watch for signs of unethical impulses within yourself. Take self-guided ethics tests to detect and address any possible propensity toward unethical behavior. Discuss any concerns with a trusted adviser or friend who can help you clarify your understanding of ethical and unethical behavior.

continued

- **Do** use situational or hypothetical questions during inter-views with HR candidates to boost your chances of selecting a leader with integrity.

- **Don't** forget to encourage your company's board of directors to provide oversight to keep HR and other executives on the straight and narrow.

- **Do** be aware that there's a fine line between confidence and arrogance. HR leaders whose rise to prominence and responsibility seems unnaturally rapid may be tempted to assume that they're exempt from ethical standards everyone else must meet.

The HR professionals you've met in this chapter have demonstrated the value that wise and ethical exercise of power, influence, and per-suasion can create for a company—and the damage that abuse of these skills can cause. Though each practitioner's story is unique in many respects, some common threads wind through the lessons these stories offer:

- The broader your business knowledge, the greater your cred-ibility—and therefore the better your chances of exerting influence.

- Influencing and persuading hinge powerfully on your ability to tie HR programs and initiatives to high-level company objectives.

- Ongoing communication with your superiors, peers, and staff is essential for identifying your company's needs and devising HR programs that offer strategic value.

- In organizations characterized by cultures in which people have limited respect for HR, you may need to behave contrary to expectations in order to demonstrate HR's value and business knowledge.

- How you wield your power, influence, and persuasion becomes even more vital during crises and tough times.

- To become an HR star, you need to carefully blend attention to leaders' and employees' emotional needs with objective facts and figures supporting your ideas.

- Misuse of power by HR professionals can be particularly damaging to company morale and productivity.

Summing Up

In this chapter, you learned about:

- Starting your new role in HR

- Building constructive relationships with higher-ups such as your boss in HR, your company's CEO, and the board of directors

- Motivating your staff to excel

- Collaborating with peers to implement valuable HR programs and ideas

- Winning buy-in for strategic HR initiatives

- Using power, influence, and persuasion to help your company recover from a crisis or survive difficult challenges

- Preventing the abuse of power by HR professionals

Leveraging Chapter Insights: Critical Questions

- Consider the many different contexts in which you exercise power, influence, and persuasion. In which of these contexts do you possess "star quality" in your use of power, influence, and persuasion? Why?

- In which of these contexts do you have difficulty wielding power, influence, and persuasion? Why? How might you strengthen your abilities in these contexts?

- With which of the contexts described in this chapter have you had little or no experience? (For example, perhaps your company has never endured a crisis or experienced a severe economic downturn. Or maybe you're about to take on a new managerial role in HR for the first time.) What steps can you take now to boost your chances of successfully exercising your power, influence, and persuasion once you begin operating in these unfamiliar circumstances?

CHAPTER ELEVEN

Enhancing and Leveraging Your Power, Influence, and Persuasion Skills

Next Steps

Key Topics Covered in This Chapter

- *Reinforcing key principles and practices in the use of power, influence, and persuasion*

- *Developing a plan for further enhancing your skills*

- *Using your skills to progress in your career as an HR professional*

C ONGRATULATIONS! You've made your way through a lot of information about the nature of power, influence, and persuasion. In this concluding chapter, we'll review key principles and practices that guide the effective, ethical use of these important HR skills. You'll also have an opportunity to develop an action plan for further strengthening these skills. In the final section of this chapter, you'll find guidelines for using these skills to move forward in your career as an HR professional. With all of this in mind, let's focus now on reviewing the core concepts and practices of power, influence, and persuasion.

Key Principles and Practices

Power, influence, and persuasion all work in concert to enable you to win buy-in for valuable HR initiatives and ideas. Yet as you learned while reading the preceding chapters in this book, each of these three mechanisms has a unique set of considerations that you need to keep in mind. Table 11-1 summarizes the most salient of these considerations.

As table 11-1 shows, power, influence, and persuasion differ in important ways. However, all three share one important characteristic: the potential for abuse. For that reason, it's vital to remember and apply these techniques for discouraging the unethical use of power, influence, and persuasion:

TABLE 11-1

Considerations in Power, Influence, and Persuasion

	Power	Influence	Persuasion
Definition	The potential to allocate resources and to make and enforce decisions.	The mechanism through which you use your power to change others' behavior or attitudes.	The process you use in trying to change or reinforce others' attitudes, opinions, or behaviors.
Example	An HR director's formal authority enables her to decide which vendor to select for an outsourcing project.	An HR director's integrity, credibility, and track record of success convince her team that her idea for a new initiative is worth supporting.	An HR director persuades a peer manager that her idea for a new initiative is worth exploring—by citing testimonials from other companies that have had good results by implementing the idea.
Benefits	Enables an organization to fulfill its basic functions, make decisions, and take action.	Enables an executive or manager to shape the behavior and attitudes of others over whom he or she has no formal authority.	Enables an executive or manager to sell his or her ideas to others by appealing to their logic and emotional needs.
Important caveats	Power has limitations: exercising formal authority may force short-term obedience but doesn't earn managers willing support from others. Power may also be abused by unscrupulous leaders to serve their own interests.	Influencers may manipulate their audience by concealing their true intentions; for example, by deliberately providing false information to gain advantage.	Persuaders may use unethical practices, such as omitting information their audience would have needed to make an informed choice about whether to support the proposed idea.
Keys to using	• Tap your positional (your place in the organizational hierarchy), relational (your connections with others), and personal (your competence and knowledge) power sources.	• Map your sphere of influence—the network of mutually dependent relationships you participate in at work. • Expand your sphere of influence by increasing your power, enhancing others' dependence on you, and opening yourself to influence by others.	• Gauge your audience's current knowledge of and receptivity to your idea. • Build a convincing business case for your idea. • Appeal to your listeners' powers of reason by selecting the right structure and evidence for your case.

(continued)

TABLE 11-1 (continued)

Considerations in Power, Influence, and Persuasion

	Power	Influence	Persuasion
Keys to using	• Understand that even though you have formal authority over others, you still depend on them for your success. • Strive to use power according to the institutional-manager style—deploying power in the service of your organization, not personal goals.	• Increase your influence through currencies of exchange—offering assistance, favors, and other forms of value to others in exchange for their cooperation. • Exert your influence by framing issues your way, presenting compelling information, acquiring technical authority, maneuvering within your organization's hierarchy, leveraging invisible social networks, and helping new leaders assimilate into the organization.	• Appeal to your listeners' emotions by using evocative language, metaphors, analogies, and stories. • Overcome resistance by identifying your audience's interests, addressing their distrust and fear, building trust, demonstrating consistency between your verbal and nonverbal messages, and addressing resisters' viewpoints before presenting your own. • Take advantage of persuasion triggers such as the law of reciprocity, social proof, and commitment and consistency. • Hone your public speaking skills—including managing stage fright, preparing for audience questions, and adapting your presentation to different learning styles.

• Align company policies and standards with the highest legal and ethical expectations.

• Zealously enforce those policies and standards.

• Include ethical performance in individual job performance reviews for your staff, while encouraging other executives and managers to do the same.

- Ensure that you and other leaders are morally equipped to use power, influence, and persuasion wisely and ethically.

- Model ethical behavior yourself in your use of power, influence, and persuasion.

Table 11-1 also affirms that the effective use of power, influence, and persuasion requires distinctive skills. As with any skill set, you may be stronger in some areas than in others. To strengthen these skills or acquire new ones, it's helpful to develop an action plan. Assessment tool 11-1 provides a worksheet for creating a plan based on your current abilities and the areas in which you need improvement.

Assessment Tool 11-1
Action Plan for Strengthening Your Power, Influence, and Persuasion Skills

Part 1: Power

1. **What are your most important sources of power?** *Consider your position in the organization, your relationships, and your personal qualities.*

2. **How will you increase your power? Document your ideas below.** *Will you enhance others' dependence on you for their success? Develop specific personal qualities, such as expertise and credibility? Work toward winning a promotion to a higher position?*

3. **In what respects, if any, are you vulnerable to the temptation to use your power to further your own interests**

continued

rather than to serve your organization? *Be honest here. Anyone who has formal power must face this question head-on to ensure ethical behavior.*

4. What steps can you take to address any vulnerabilities you noted in question 3? *For example, are there internal auditing procedures that can be established to remove temptations among all leaders to abuse their power?*

Part 2: Influence

1. If you've mapped your sphere of influence, what steps might you take to expand your sphere? *Will you enhance your formal power? Increase others' dependencies on you? Open yourself more to others' influence?*

2. How might you use currencies of exchange more effectively to extend your influence in your organization? *Do you need to learn more about what kinds of favors and support others in your organization value? If so, how will you gather that information? How will you provide those currencies? And which currencies will you strive to get in return?*

3. Which tactics of influence do you need to practice most in order to strengthen your skills? *Consider the following mechanisms: framing issues your way, influencing others through savvy use of information, influencing through*

technical authority, maneuvering within your company's report-
ing hierarchy, leveraging invisible social networks, and assimi-
lating new leaders.

4. What steps will you take to practice the tactics of
influence you listed in question 3? *For instance, will you*
acquire more specialized knowledge of HR information tech-
nology? Will you work on expanding the social networks in
which you participate?

5. In what ways, if any, might you be tempted to use your
influence unethically? *For example, have you felt tempted in*
the past to distort information deliberately in order to manipu-
late others?

6. How might you remove any temptation to use influence unethically? *For example, could you commit to exam-*
ining the information you present to others and ensuring that
the data is objective and complete?

Part 3: Persuasion

1. Which elements of persuasion pose the greatest difficulty for you? *For example, do you need to strengthen your*
personal credibility or form a more thorough understanding of
your audience? Do you have difficulty constructing a solid case

continued

for your ideas? Would you benefit from stronger communication skills?

2. What steps will you take to strengthen the weak areas you identified in question 1? *For instance, will you acquire new expertise in order to build your credibility? Commit to talking with several audience members before giving a presentation, to gauge their concerns and receptivity to your ideas? Practice an upcoming presentation with a trusted colleague who will give his or her impressions of your case?*

3. Which of your presentation skills need to be improved? *Do you have trouble making the most of graphics? Are you overwhelmed by presentation anxiety? Do you find it relatively easy to structure your presentations effectively?*

4. What actions can you take to strengthen the presentation skills you listed in question 3? *For example, could you prepare a checklist to ensure that you've covered all the bases—such as including a compelling opening, using effective graphics, controlling stage fright, and so forth?*

Using Your Power, Influence, and Persuasion Skills to Move Forward in Your Career

No matter what level you've achieved in the HR field, you'll need to continually learn and grow. Why? Change is a constant in the business arena. Professionals who open themselves to constant learning and who continually burnish their skills offer more value to their organizations by helping them adapt to change and make effective strategic decisions. Savvy and ethical use of your power, as well as your influence and persuasion skills, can help you progress to higher positions and greater levels of responsibility.

According to one study, more HR professionals than ever are climbing into the ranks of senior-level management.[1] Some have been promoted to positions such as chief executive officer, chief operating officer, president, and chairman. One driver of HR practitioners' ascent into the executive suites is heightened awareness among business leaders that employees constitute one of a company's strongest competitive advantages. Indeed, for many enterprises, HR issues head the list of priorities discussed during strategy formulation sessions.

How can you use your power, influence, and persuasion to achieve increasingly higher levels of responsibility? One way is to boost your personal power and your influence by strengthening your business and strategic expertise and knowledge. The experts offer numerous suggestions:[2]

- **Develop a strategic mind-set.** Understand your company's high-level strategic aims. How does it plan to beat rivals? Then learn how the various parts of your organization (especially finance, marketing, sales, operations, and accounting) interact and serve the corporate strategy. To acquire this knowledge, participate in these functions' strategic planning sessions, as well as in interdepartmental task forces. Also assess the culture of each function; each one will have distinctive priorities and ways of operating. Discern cross-functional rivalries, and facilitate positive interactions among the various groups.

- **Help your company execute its strategy.** That means analyzing the long-term impact of HR decisions on your company's ability to compete in its industry. For example, if your organization's strategy hinges on changing its sales-force model from individual sales calls to a greater reliance on direct mail, you'll need to make changes in sales-force compensation and staffing, IT staffing, and training programs.

- **Mold senior executives into an effective team.** Your CEO relies on his or her chief HR officer to help meld the company's senior executives (including the CEO) into a top-notch team. To provide that assistance, develop a keen understanding of each officer's core needs and concerns. Spend time alone with each officer to glean these insights. Facilitate executive meetings in ways that enable participants to generate creative ideas and remain focused on big-picture strategic concerns.

- **Put your company's needs first.** Every time you present a proposal or frame an argument, explain clearly how your organization—especially its bottom line—will benefit from implementing your suggestion. Provide plenty of data and objective information to back up your suggestions and decisions.

- **Gain cross-functional and broad business knowledge and experience.** Develop your non-HR knowledge and skills by attending courses and seminars, reading general-business books, and taking some detours from a straight-line HR career path. Lateral moves and rotating job assignments in different kinds of companies and different functions within the same company can help. Line positions with profit-and-loss responsibility can prove very valuable.

- **Build a reputation for action.** Show that you can learn and recover from failures by creating alternative plans. Demonstrate that you can act decisively and take risks. Take on problems that others are afraid of or that cause the biggest organizational headaches.

You can enhance your relational power and your influence by applying the following practices:

- **Build diverse connections.** Strive for diversity in the relationships you establish. For example, get to know people in all areas of your organization. Seek out people whom you know to have a wide variety of opinions. People the committees you form with individuals who have dissenting viewpoints. And understand the views and needs of the people you collaborate with throughout the organization. The broader your perspective, the more you'll be able to read your organization and formulate proposals and recommendations that will win support. Also, building diverse connections is a kind of insurance: you never know whose support you may need in the future!

- **Demonstrate trustworthiness.** Win others' trust in you by fulfilling promises and commitments, treating others fairly, and demonstrating concern for others' well-being. Be dependable and helpful to others—particularly during difficult times. And trust others; you'll inspire their trust in you.

- **Strengthen your emotional intelligence.** Separate personal feelings from workplace issues. Be aware of your emotional triggers, and monitor your feelings so that they don't interfere with your ability to make decisions, evaluate ideas, and implement plans. Look beyond any fears or insecurities and embrace daunting challenges anyway. If needed, join positive support groups or ask a coach to help you sharpen your emotional self-awareness and monitor your feelings and their impact.

Finally, you can strengthen your persuasive powers through the following practices:

- **Learn to speak your audience's language.** For example, to persuade your CFO to fund an HR initiative, explain the initiative's benefits in language he or she speaks—such as "return on investment," "payback period," "failure rate," "cost per unit of service," "people dollars required per production unit," and "competitive advantage."

- **Frame proposals in terms of "why," not "what."** To succeed at the HR executive level, you need to know why a particular idea or initiative must be implemented or why it will generate value for your company. Presidents and CEOs grapple with the "why" constantly while making decisions. They rely on those below them to handle the "what" (such as which resources will be needed) and "how" (for example, the processes by which an initiative will be carried out).

- **Strengthen your public speaking skills.** Sharpen your ability to deliver compelling presentations to groups of executives— by joining organizations such as Toastmasters, asking a friend or trusted colleague to help you rehearse an important presenta- tion, or reading guidebooks on public speaking.

Applying all of these practices may sound like a lot of work, but the results make the effort worthwhile. Consider the story of Anne Szostak, chairman and CEO of Fleet Rhode Island, a bank based in Providence, Rhode Island, and executive vice president and director of HR and diversity at FleetBoston Financial Corporation:[3]

As head of Fleet Rhode Island, Anne Szostak has responsibility for a forty-eight-branch banking operation that employs four thousand people. She leads Fleet's business, government relations, and corporate giving in Rhode Island. She also leads HR and diversity for Fleet Rhode Island's parent company, FleetBoston Financial—the nation's seventh-largest financial holding company.

Szostak's first job was as a corporate training director for a retailer. During her thirty-year career at Fleet, she has held several executive posts—including chairman, president, and CEO of Fleet Maine; executive VP of consumer banking; and senior VP of bank operations.

Looking back over her career, Szostak maintains that serving in various line-management roles has helped her to better understand the business's issues. She learned the impact of profit and loss, which helped her take on additional leadership roles in the company. Her advice to other HR professionals seeking to further their careers? "Understand the business inside and out—talking the language is terribly important." Szostak also advocates developing relationships with several mentors—building "a little advisory board for yourself." Today, she has a set of about six people whom she regularly taps for advice and impressions.

In addition, Szostak recommends taking initiative. For instance, when she became the HR director at Fleet, she benchmarked other companies without any directive from above. She also built employee programs to prepare Fleet to apply for a spot on Working Mother *magazine's annual list of the 100 best companies for working mothers. Fleet made the list. Szostak describes this achievement as a turning point: "Seventy-five percent of our employees are women, and I was determined to make it easier for employees to be able to combine work and family," she notes.*

Szostak's additional recommendations to HR practitioners include being cognizant of industry and national trends, building credibility, and taking risks. "Trust your instincts," she adds. "Work hard but play smart, keep criticisms to yourself, and keep a sense of humor."

Summing Up

This chapter helped you:

- Review key principles and practices for the ethical and effective use of power, influence, and persuasion. Because the potential for abuse is common across all three mechanisms, you saw a review of strategies for preventing such abuse.

- Develop a plan for strengthening your skills in these areas—including identifying areas for improvement and addressing vulnerabilities regarding improper use of these mechanisms.

- Discover ways to use your power, influence, and persuasion to move forward in your career as an HR professional. Several case studies, as well as a set of guidelines for each of the three mechanisms, were provided. Broad business experience and a strategic mind-set seem particularly vital to achieving higher levels of responsibility.

Leveraging Chapter Insights: Critical Questions

- What role do you currently occupy in your organization? What levels would you like to achieve in your career?

- Which of the practices described in this chapter would be most helpful for advancing your career to the level you desire?

- How will you begin applying those practices?

Leading When You're Not the Boss

As an HR professional, you may sometimes find yourself in situations where you have management or leadership responsibility but no corresponding formal authority. For example, perhaps you head up a cross-functional team tasked with developing a new performance-management system, and some or all of the team's members don't report to you. Or maybe you participate along with your CEO and other executives in the company's strategic planning process. In these and similar cases, issuing direct orders is not feasible. Nevertheless, you must lead.

True leadership, of course, has never been a matter of formal authority. Leaders become effective when the people around them acknowledge them as leaders because of their personal qualities: their attributes, attitudes, and behaviors.

There is no single best way to lead when you're not the boss. Different situations—a crisis, a long-term project, and so forth—call for different types of leaders. Nevertheless, the five-step approach outlined in this appendix can help you in many situations when you do not have a boss-subordinate relationship with others. This approach was developed by Harvard negotiation specialist Roger Fisher and his colleague Alan Sharp. Both men contend that their approach can be applied to virtually any project, team, or meeting in which you are a participant.

Step 1: Establish Goals

People accomplish the most when their objectives are clear. It follows that any group's first order of business should be to write down exactly what it hopes to achieve. The person who asks the question "Can we start by clarifying our goals?" and who then assumes the lead in discussing and drafting those goals is taking a leadership role, whatever his or her formal position.

Step 2: Think Systematically

Observe your next meeting: do the participants immediately plunge into the issue at hand and start arguing over what to do? If so, the meeting needs more systematic leadership. Effective leaders gather and lay out the pertinent data, seek out the causes of the situation, and propose actions based on their analysis. By engaging group members in this type of systematic approach and guiding them through it, you become a de facto leader. You keep people focused on the problem-solving process, and you reinforce your leadership by asking appropriate questions such as the following:

- Do we have all the information we need to analyze this situation?

- Can we focus on the causes of the problem we're trying to solve?

Once you've determined the cause of the problem, you can lead people in a similar systematic discussion of potential solutions.

Step 3: Learn from Experience—While It's Happening

Most teams plow ahead on a project, and only when it's over do they conduct an after-action review to reflect on what they have learned. But sometimes it's more effective to learn as you go along. This means that part of a group's daily work is to conduct mini-reviews and make any necessary midcourse corrections.

Why is this ongoing process more effective than an after-action review? The answer is that the data is fresh in everyone's mind. The reviews engage people's attention because the group can use its conclusions to make adjustments. Here, too, you can play a de facto leadership role by focusing the group on regular review and learning.

Step 4: Engage Others

Successful groups engage the skills and efforts of every member. This doesn't happen naturally; someone must make it happen. You can step into this leadership role by seeking the best fit possible between members' interests and skills and the tasks that need doing. List all the tasks that need doing, and match them with individuals or subgroups. If no one wants a particular task, brainstorm ways to make it more interesting or challenging. Partition the task if necessary into small parts that others can manage. Also, draw out the group's quieter members so that everyone feels like part of the team.

Step 5: Provide Feedback

Even if you're not the boss, you can provide helpful feedback. Simply indicating your appreciation of the efforts of others—"I thought you did a great job in there"—will cost you nothing but will win people to your side.

Given the popularity of teams, HR managers at every level can find opportunities to act as leaders without formal authority. Use those opportunities whenever you confront a leadership vacuum or whenever stepping forward can improve a situation. The experience you develop in such situations will help you increase your personal power and improve your effectiveness as a manager and leader. Always remember, if you learn to lead successfully *without* formal authority, leading *with* it will be easy.

Implementation Tools

This appendix contains tools for assessing an audience that you need to persuade and gauging your own personal ability to persuade others.

Understanding Your Audience

How can you assess and persuade your audience? Use the worksheet in figure B-1 to clarify the main points of your proposal and assess the audience you are trying to influence and persuade.

Assessing Your Persuasion Skills

Use the tool in figure B-2 to assess your persuasion abilities.

FIGURE B-1

Assessing Your Audience

Use this tool to assess an audience that you will need to persuade.

Part I: Description of Your Proposal and Its Benefits

What is the idea or proposition that you plan to communicate to your audience?

What do you hope to persuade your audience to do based on that idea or proposition?

List the benefits of your idea or proposition.

Part II: Audience Assessment

1. *In the first column, list the names of the people whom you will need to persuade. These individuals will include the following:*
   - *Decision makers—individuals who approve or reject your idea*
   - *Stakeholders—people who are affected by acceptance of your proposal*
   - *Influencers—people who have access to the stakeholders and decision makers and can sway their opinions*
2. *In the second column, list the benefits that you think each audience member values most.*
3. *In the third column, note how you would gauge each audience member's receptivity to your idea. Which individuals are hostile, supportive, uninterested, uninformed, or neutral?*
4. *In the fourth column, list each audience member's preferred decision-making style. For example, which individuals want a lot of factual information before making a decision? Which ones prefer to analyze other respected individuals' decisions and follow their lead? Which ones tend to feel enthusiastic about new ideas early on but then look for data to support the proposed idea? Which ones, in general, are initially skeptical of others' ideas?*

Name	Benefits	Receptivity to Your Idea	Decision-Making Style
Decision Makers			
Stakeholders			
Influencers			

Part III: Action Planning

1. *In the first column, copy the names of the individuals just as you listed them in Part II.*

2. *In the second column, note how you plan to win each audience member's mind. That is, what benefits of your idea will you emphasize? What evidence will you provide to reassure your audience that those benefits are within their reach? What words will you use?*

3. *In the third column, note how you plan to win each audience member's heart. That is, what vivid descriptions, metaphors, analogies, and stories might you provide to connect with your listeners on an emotional level?*

4. *In the fourth column, note how you plan to acknowledge resisters' concerns and communicate your understanding of their concerns.*

Name	Actions to Win Minds	Actions to Win Hearts	Actions to Deal with Resistance
Decision Makers			
Stakeholders			
Influencers			

Part IV: Activating Triggers and Audience Self-Persuasion

What persuasion triggers might you set in motion before your presentation? For example, if you think the reciprocity trigger might increase your persuasiveness, what favors or kindnesses might you do for your audience members that would boost the likelihood that they'll support your idea in return?

How might you activate audience self-persuasion during your presentation? For example, what disturbing, leading, and rhetorical questions might you pose to encourage listeners to persuade *themselves* of the value of your idea?

Source: Harvard ManageMentor. Adapted with permission.

Assessing Your Ability to Persuade

Part I: Assessment

Use this tool to assess your persuasion abilities. For each statement below, indicate how accurately the statement describes you. "1" indicates "Not true," "5" indicates "Very true." Be sure to answer based on your actual behavior in real workplace situations. In that way, you'll have the most accurate assessment of your skills.

Statement	Rating Not true				Very true
1. I appropriately establish my qualifications before I try to persuade.	1	2	3	4	5
2. When persuading, I offer proof of how people have been able to trust me in the past.	1	2	3	4	5
3. I analyze listeners' words and behavior to assess their decision-making style and receptivity.	1	2	3	4	5
4. When persuading, I describe the benefits and unique aspects of my idea.	1	2	3	4	5
5. I use metaphors, analogies, and stories in my presentations to highlight my key points.	1	2	3	4	5
6. I consciously limit the number of points I make in my presentations to no more than three or four.	1	2	3	4	5
7. I support my arguments with highly credible evidence.	1	2	3	4	5
8. When I cite facts, data, or statistics, I package the information for clarity and memorability.	1	2	3	4	5
9. I encourage feedback from my listeners to activate audience self-persuasion.	1	2	3	4	5
10. I use disturbing, leading, and rhetorical questions to encourage audience self-persuasion.	1	2	3	4	5
11. I actively listen to my audience and reflect the content and emotions behind their statements.	1	2	3	4	5
12. I analyze my audience before persuading, to determine my strategy.	1	2	3	4	5
13. I tailor my persuasion strategy, material, and approach to different audiences.	1	2	3	4	5
14. I vary my choice of media according to the message I want to communicate.	1	2	3	4	5
15. I consciously help others in an effort to build trust and credibility, knowing that this may result in a relationship in which others want to help me later.	1	2	3	4	5
16. I try to encourage people to make their commitments to my ideas publicly or on paper.	1	2	3	4	5

Statement	Rating				
	Not true				*Very true*
17. I consciously tap the power that comes from titles or positions of authority that I hold.	1	2	3	4	5
18. When I possess exclusive information, I emphasize its scarcity value to those I'm persuading.	1	2	3	4	5
19. When I promote something, I stress that it's standard practice or part of a popular trend.	1	2	3	4	5
20. I associate myself with products, people, or companies that my audience admires.	1	2	3	4	5
21. I emphasize the similarities I share with people I want to persuade.	1	2	3	4	5
22. When I encounter resistance to my idea, I use paraphrasing and questioning to understand the source of the resistance and to communicate my understanding of the resisters' concerns.	1	2	3	4	5
23. I try to establish positive relationships and feelings with people I want to persuade.	1	2	3	4	5
24. When I anticipate encountering resistance to my ideas, I raise and understand opponents' arguments before presenting my own views.	1	2	3	4	5
25. I use affirmative, assertive speech and win-win language while persuading.	1	2	3	4	5
Score for each column					

Total score

(Calculate your score by adding up the numbers in all your responses.)

Part II: Scoring

Use the following table to interpret your score.

104–125	**Exceptional:** You're a talented persuader with a solid understanding of the art and science of persuasion.
78–103	**Superior:** You're a highly effective persuader in many areas but would benefit from refining some of your skills.
51–77	**Adequate:** You know and practice many of the basics of persuasion. However, you can increase your success by further extending your skills.
25–50	**Deficient:** You'll need to work broadly on your persuasion skills to begin changing or reinforcing others' attitudes, beliefs, and behaviors.

Source: Adapted from Harry Mills, *Artful Persuasion: How to Command Attention, Change Minds, and Influence People* (New York: AMACOM, 2000). Used with permission.

Leveraging Your Social Network

Use the worksheet in figure C-1 to help you map your social network and identify ways to strengthen it.

FIGURE C-1

A Brief Personal Network Assessment

Step 1

Write down the names of people you rely on for information or problem solving to do your work. These people can come from any and all walks of life.

Names

Step 2

List the number of relationships that fall into each category for the major descriptors below.

	Group
1 = within same group	
2 = outside group, within same business unit	
3 = outside business unit, within same division	
4 = outside division, within same organization	
5 = different organization	

	Proximity
1 = works immediately next to me	
2 = same floor	
3 = different floor	
4 = different building	
5 = different city	
6 = different country	

	Interaction
1 = never	
2 = seldom	
3 = sometimes	
4 = frequently	
5 = very frequently	

	Effort
1 = 1 hour or less per month	
2 = 2–3 hours per month	
3 = 1 hour per week	
4 = 2–3 hours per week	
5 = 1 hour or more per day	

	Time Known
1 = less than 1 year	
2 = 1–3 years	
3 = 3–5 years	
4 = 5–10 years	
5 = 10+ years	

	Hierarchy
1 = higher than yours	
2 = equal to yours	
3 = lower than yours	
4 = not applicable	

	Primary Medium
1 = unplanned face-to-face meetings	
2 = planned face-to-face meetings	
3 = telephone	
4 = e-mail	
5 = instant messaging	

	Gender
1 = same	
2 = different	

	Age
1 = younger by 6 years or more	
2 = your age plus or minus 5 years	
3 = older by more than 6 years	

	Ethnicity
1 = same ethnicity	
2 = different ethnicity	

continued

Step 3

Take a look at the composition of your network and identify biases that may affect how you do your job. For example, do you have a tendency to go only to people who are accessible to you rather than to those who may have more relevant information? Note implications these biases have for the way you do your work and actions you can take to resolve these issues.

Bias	Implication/Action

Step 4

Identify up to eight skills or types of expertise necessary for you to do your job. For example, types of expertise can be technical, such as programming skills; administrative, such as knowledge of company-specific databases and software; or managerial, such as program management or leadership skills.

Expertise you need to do your work
1.
2.
3.
4.
5.
6.
7.
8.

Step 5

Transfer the types of expertise to the first row and the people in your personal network to the first column of the table below. (The number of rows can be expanded as appropriate.) Then indicate with a check mark which people you go to for which types of expertise in each of the rows. Finally, tally the number of check marks across each row and down each column.

Name	Exp. 1	Exp. 2	Exp. 3	Exp. 4	Exp. 5	Exp. 6	Exp. 7	Exp. 8	Total
1.									
2.									
3.									
4.									
5.									
6.									
7.									
8.									
9.									
10.									
Total									

Step 6

Review the scores in step 5 for each of the people in your expertise network to see if there are people you are overly dependent on or people you do not leverage sufficiently (or possibly leverage for the wrong kinds of tasks). Next, review the scores for each type of expertise. Are there types of expertise you need to further develop but do not have a set of relationships to help on this front? Finally, note implications of the expertise gaps and overdependencies to the way you do your work. Indicate what actions you can take to resolve these issues.

Expertise Gap/Overdependency	Implication/Action

Source: Rob Cross and Andrew Parker, *The Hidden Power of Social Networks: Understand How Work Really Gets Done* (Boston: Harvard Business School Press, 2004), 167–171. Used with permission.

Commonsense Rules for Presentation Visuals

Formal presentations are an important tool of persuasion for today's HR practitioner. Visual images containing text or graphics have become a standard feature in these presentations, so it is imperative that you master them.

Numerous software programs have made it possible for business-people to enhance their presentations with eye-catching text, charts, and graphs. The programs offer many color and design features—including three-dimensional effects, many font choices, clip art, and much more.

When used judiciously, these programs let you create visuals that convey more information in less time than you could by using more traditionally prepared visual aids. With high-tech visuals, you can get key points across and make them memorable. Used carelessly, however, these powerful tools can confuse or bore your audience, diminishing the impact of your entire presentation. Here are a few rules for making the most of your presentation visuals.

Rule 1: Subordinate Your Visuals to Your Message

You and what you have to say should always be the focus of the presentation. Visuals should therefore play a supportive role. They should never command center stage. You can observe this important rule by following these guidelines:

- Don't try to say everything through overheads.

- Refrain from simply reading your overheads to the audience.

- Avoid visuals that are not essential to your presentation.

Rule 2: Keep Your Visuals Simple

Some presenters clutter every overhead with border-to-border text, as in example A. Extra words detract from the presenter's message and make the audience work unnecessarily hard to capture key points.

Example A is overburdened with text. It contains information that would be better conveyed verbally by the speaker. Example B, in contrast, captures the key points without the supporting details. These points are clear and easy to remember.

EXAMPLE A [CLUTTERED]

Challenges for the Coming Year

> The sales force must become more efficient next year. Currently, selling costs are running close to 20 percent of revenues. The industry average is 14 percent.
> On average, we have fifteen days of finished goods inventory. Financing and maintaining that inventory are expensive. If we were better at forecasting sales, we could cut that inventory level—perhaps by as much as four days. That would save the company close to $50,000 per year.
> Our workforce needs more training to stay competitive. We should aim for forty hours of training for all nonprofessional employees and sixty hours for professional employees.

EXAMPLE B [SIMPLE]

Challenges for the Coming Year

- Greater sales efficiency
- Less finished goods inventory
- More training for everyone

Source: *Power, Influence, and Persuasion*, Harvard Business Essentials (Boston: Harvard Business School Press, 2005), 142. Used with permission.

Rule 3: Use a Minimum of Devices

People who take the time to master presentation software are tempted to use many of these applications' cool devices: different colors, many font styles and sizes, shading, and on and on. Don't fall into this trap. Those devices can deflect attention from the message. Ask yourself, "Do I need the fancy fill effects and the clip art? Would one font style be better than the three I'm using?" In most cases, your visuals will look more professional if you use a bare minimum of devices. Simpler is usually better—as you can see by comparing examples C and D (two presentation slides). Note that example C uses too many variations of shadings, fonts, and type treatments, as well as too much clip art. The slide is overwhelming visually. Example D presents information in a much cleaner format that's easy on

EXAMPLE C

Cluttered Visual

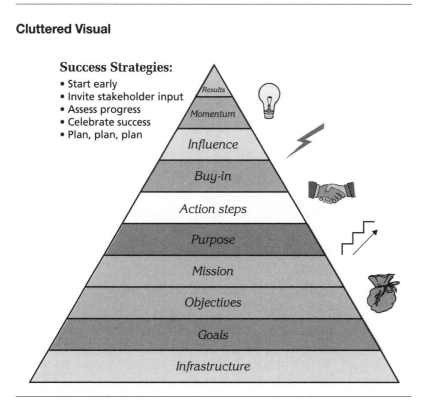

EXAMPLE D

Simple Visual

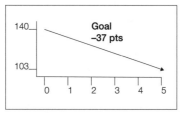

Year	Improve Productivity	Focus on Target Markets	Align Business Units	Upgrade IT	Total
1					
2	−11	−6			−17
3			−4	−2	−6
4			−4	−5	−9
5			−2	−3	−5
Total	−11 pts	−6 pts	−10 pts	−10 pts	−37 pts

Source: Adapted from Robert S. Kaplan and David P. Norton, *Strategy Maps* (Boston: Harvard Business School Press, 2004), 371. Used with permission.

the eyes. No fancy shading, varied typography, or clip art was needed to convey the information shown in this slide.

Rule 4: Make Your Images Large and Legible

Your visuals should be clearly legible to everyone in the room—even those in the back row of seats. If you've observed rules 2 and 3, then you'll have plenty of room on each slide or overhead to make your images large.

Rule 5: Use Graphics to Tell Key Parts of the Story

Most people are visually oriented. They perceive and digest information best when it's presented graphically. For example, suppose you want to

FIGURE D-1

Presenting Recruiting-Method Performance Graphically

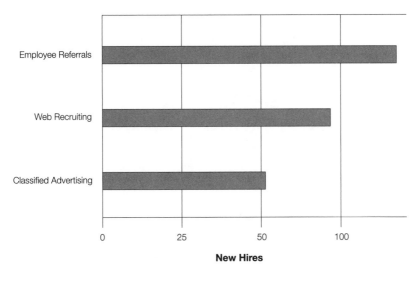

New Hires

Source: Adapted from *Power, Influence, and Persuasion,* Harvard Business Essentials (Boston: Harvard Business School Press, 2005), 144. Used with permission.

make the point that one recruiting method—the employee referral program you initiated—has proved less expensive and more effective than two other methods: classified advertising and Internet recruiting. You could simply tell your audience, "Results for the previous twelve months indicate that employee referrals brought in more high-quality new hires than advertising and Web recruiting." You could also put this same information on an overhead sheet containing the following sentence: "Employee referrals outperformed advertising and Web recruiting during the past twelve months." You could then go on to provide details about the relative performance of these three methods.

Alternatively, you could use a graphic image that shows the relative performance of the three methods (figure D-1).

To create the greatest impact, reserve graphics like those in figure D-1 for the key points of your presentation. If you create visuals for everything, you'll lose the key points in the clutter.

Rule 6: Use the Most Appropriate Graphic Form

Most presentation programs and their spreadsheet supporting systems allow you to produce pie charts, column charts, bar charts, line charts, scattergrams, and so forth. Each is best for presenting certain types of data.

Pie Charts

Pie charts are best when your goal is to show the impact of different factors on the whole. Thus, if you wanted your audience to understand the contributions of your company's three recruiting methods to total hiring, a pie chart would be your best choice (figure D-2). Each method is shown as a slice of the entire pie.

Bar and Column Charts

Use bar and column charts when you want the audience to compare outcomes, such as in the chart shown earlier in figure D-1. In that chart, the audience can see *both* the relative performances of the three recruiting methods and the number of new hires that each generated. That's something they won't see as readily in a pie chart.

FIGURE D-2

Using a Pie Chart to Show the Effect of Parts on the Whole

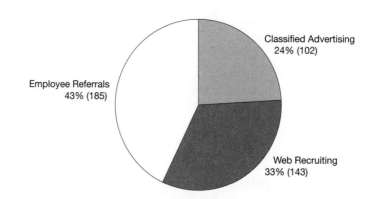

Classified Advertising
24% (102)

Employee Referrals
43% (185)

Web Recruiting
33% (143)

Source: Adapted from *Power, Influence, and Persuasion,* Harvard Business Essentials (Boston: Harvard Business School Press, 2005), 145. Used with permission.

Line Charts

Line charts are particularly good for indicating trends. In figure D–3, we show the change in one company's employee turnover rate over time—January through December 2005. If we were comparing this organization's turnover trend to that of a competitor, we could easily put them on the same chart.

Scattergrams

If you want to show a statistical linear regression (the best fit of a line drawn through a number of scattered data points), exponential smoothing, or a moving average, a scattergram is your best bet. These charts are invaluable when you have many data points for one specific variable—for example, the employee turnover rates in fifty branch stores for each month of a year. Figure D–4 maps data points

FIGURE D-3

Using a Line Chart to Show Change Over Time

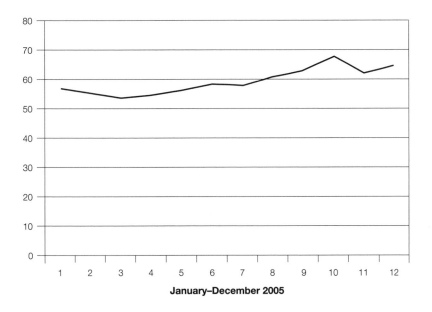

January–December 2005

Source: Adapted from *Power, Influence, and Persuasion,* Harvard Business Essentials (Boston: Harvard Business School Press, 2005), 146. Used with permission.

FIGURE D-4

Scattergram with Linear Trend Line

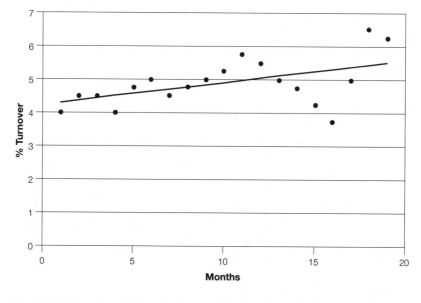

Source: Adapted from *Power, Influence, and Persuasion,* Harvard Business Essentials (Boston: Harvard Business School Press, 2005), 147. Used with permission.

along the x (time) and y (turnover) axes. In the figure, we created a best-fit trend line based on statistical linear regression for turnover rates over eighteen months. The audience can see at a glance the direction that turnover rates are taking, even though the monthly percentage returns are scattered around that trend.

Rule 7: Label the Key Features of Your Graphics

Make sure your audience will understand at a glance what the quantitative data in your graphics represent. For example, the top graph in figure D-5 shows data for a particular company. But what does each column represent? And what do the values on the vertical axis mean?

In the labeled version of the same chart in figure D-5, the audience can now see that each column represents the dollar value of Acme

FIGURE D-5

Labels Help Clarify Data

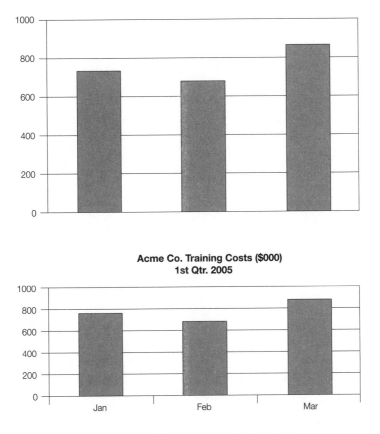

Source: Adapted from *Power, Influence, and Persuasion,* Harvard Business Essentials (Boston: Harvard Business School Press, 2005), 148. Used with permission.

Company's training costs, expressed in thousands, for the first three months of 2005.

With the availability of graphics software, it has become easier than ever to prepare illustrations for your presentations. If you observe these seven rules for the use of graphics, your presentations will be more professional and more effective.

Notes

Introduction

1. John P. Kotter, "Power, Dependence, and Effective Management," *Harvard Business Review,* July–August 1977, 125–126.

Chapter 1

1. Lisbeth Claus and Jessica Collison, "The Maturing Profession of Human Resources in the United States of America Survey Report," *SHRM Research,* January 2004, vi, vii, ix, 5, 8.

2. Susan Meisinger, "When You Talk, Do People Listen?" *HR Magazine,* September 2003.

3. Ibid.

4. Wayne Brockbank and Dave Ulrich, *Competencies for the New HR* (Alexandria, VA: University of Michigan Business School, Society for Human Resource Management, and Global Consulting Alliance, 2003), 33–34, 63–67.

5. Claus and Collison, "The Maturing Profession," 14.

6. Lin Grensing-Pophal, "Are You Promotable? What Does It Take to Succeed in HR?" SHRM white paper, Society for Human Resource Management, Alexandria, VA, July 2001.

7. Dave Patel, "Proactive Personality Contributes to Career Success," SHRM research report, Society for Human Resource Management, Alexandria, VA, May 2002.

Chapter 2

1. Rosabeth Moss Kanter, "Power Failure in Management Circuits," *Harvard Business Review,* July–August 1979, 65.

2. Ibid.

3. Jeffrey Pfeffer, *Managing with Power* (Boston: Harvard Business School Press, 1992), 9.

4. David C. McClelland and David H. Burnham, "Power Is the Great Motivator," *Harvard Business Review,* January 2003, 117–126. This section draws heavily on this source.

5. Ibid.

Chapter 3

1. John P. Kotter, "Power, Dependency, and Effective Management," *Harvard Business Review,* July–August 1977, 128.

2. For an expanded treatment of Deming's role in reshaping postwar Japan, see Richard Luecke, *Scuttle Your Ships Before Advancing* (New York: Oxford University Press, 1994), 64–76.

3. Jeffrey Pfeffer, *Managing with Power* (Boston: Harvard Business School Press, 1992), 63–64.

4. Susan J. Wells, "Five Who Have Made It," *HR Magazine,* June 2003.

Chapter 4

1. B. Kim Barnes, *Exercising Influence* (Berkeley, CA: Barnes & Conti Associates, 2000), 9.

2. For the details of this story, see Gregory H. Watson, *Strategic Benchmarking* (New York: John Wiley & Sons, 1993), 129–148.

3. Allan R. Cohen and David L. Bradford, *Influence Without Authority* (New York: John Wiley & Sons, 1989), 73.

Chapter 5

1. Jeffrey Pfeffer, *Managing with Power* (Boston: Harvard Business School Press, 1992), 203.

2. Adapted from Susan J. Wells, "Finding the Best Medicine," *HR Magazine,* January 2002.

3. Thomas Johnson and Robert Kaplan, *Relevance Lost: The Decline and Fall of Management Accounting* (Boston: Harvard Business School Press, 1987).

4. Harold J. Leavitt, *Top Down: Why Hierarchies Are Here to Stay and How to Manage Them More Effectively* (Boston: Harvard Business School Press, 2004), chapters 8 and 9. The subsections on pathfinding, problem solving, and implementing are adapted from this book.

5. Rob Cross and Andrew Parker, *The Hidden Power of Social Networks: Understanding How Work Really Gets Done in Organizations* (Boston: Harvard Business School Press, 2004), chapter 6.

6. Keith Rolla, Salvatore Parise, and Rob Cross, "Getting New Hires Up to Speed Quickly," *MIT Sloan Management Review,* Winter 2005, 35–41.

7. This section draws from Diane Downey, *Assimilating New Leaders: The Key to Executive Retention* (New York: AMACOM, 2001), 5, 237–239.

Chapter 6

1. This chapter draws heavily on material found in the Persuasion module of Harvard ManageMentor®, an online product of Harvard Business School Publishing.

2. These questions were contributed by Professor Kathleen Reardon. They are from the inventory of persuasive skills found in her book *It's All Politics* (New York: Currency/Doubleday, 2005).

3. Michael D. Watkins, "The Power to Persuade," Note 9-800-323 (Boston: Harvard Business School Publishing, July 24, 2000).

Chapter 7

1. This chapter draws heavily on material found in the Persuasion module of Harvard ManageMentor®, an online product of Harvard Business School Publishing.

2. Adapted with permission from Shelle Rose Charvet, *Words That Change Minds: Mastering the Language of Influence,* 2nd ed. (Dubuque, IA: Kendall/Hunt, 1997), 21, 37, 55, 98, 113, 120, 136.

3. Persuasion triggers were first developed and explained by Robert B. Cialdini in his article "Harnessing the Science of Persuasion," *Harvard Business Review,* OnPoint Enhanced Edition, October 2001, 72–79. The material on this topic presented in this chapter is adapted from this source.

Chapter 8

1. The discussion of the Greek method of presentation is adapted from "Presentations and the Ancient Greeks," *Harvard Management Communication Letter,* January 1999, 5–8.

2. This section on the styles of learning is adapted from "Presentations That Appeal to All of Your Listeners," *Harvard Management Communication Letter,* June 2000, 4–5.

3. The following subsections are adapted from Constantine Von Hoffman, Richard Bierck, Michael Hattersley, and Nick Wreden, "Handling Q&A: The Five Kinds of Listening," *Harvard Management Update 2* (February 1999).

4. This section is drawn from John Daly and Isa Engleberg, "Coping with Stage Fright," *Presentations That Motivate and Persuade,* The Results-Driven Manager Series (Boston: Harvard Business School Press, 2004), 49–58.

Chapter 9

1. Philip G. Zimbardo, "Power Turns Good Soldiers into Bad Apples," *The Boston Globe,* May 9, 2004, http://www.boston.com/news/globe/ editorial_opinion/oped/articles/2004/05/09/power_turns_good_soldiers_ into_bad_apples.

2. As told in Richard Leifer, Christopher McDermott, Gina Colarelli O'Connor, Lois Peters, Mark Rice, and Robert Veryzer, *Radical Innovation* (Boston: Harvard Business School Press, 2000), 56–57.

3. Paraphrased from Peter Elkind, "The Fall of the House of Grasso," *Fortune,* October 18, 2004, 286–310.

4. Joseph L. Badaracco Jr. and Allen P. Weber, "Business Ethics: A View from the Trenches," *California Management Review* 37, no. 2 (Winter 1995), 8–9.

5. Allan R. Cohen and David L. Bradford, *Influence Without Authority* (New York: John Wiley & Sons, 1991), ix.

6. Ibid., x.

7. Steve Bates, "Corporate Ethics Undergoing Historic Change," *HR News,* June 29, 2004.

8. Joshua Joseph and Evren Esen, *SHRM/Ethics Resource Center 2003 Business Ethics Survey* (Alexandria, VA: Society for Human Resource Management, 2003), 4–5.

9. Ibid.

10. Dale Buss, "Corporate Compasses," *HR Magazine,* June 2004.

Chapter 10

1. Adapted from Ann Pomeroy, "An Action-Driven HR Leader," *HR Magazine,* October 2004.

2. Adapted from Pamela Babcock, "Throwing the Switch," *HR Magazine,* December 2003.

3. This section is adapted from Lawrence Richter Quinn, "Backing Up the Board," *HR Magazine,* June 2004.

4. Adapted from Kelly Mollica, "Perceptions of Fairness," *HR Magazine,* June 2004.

5. Adapted from Bill Roberts, "Side by Side," *HR Magazine,* March 2004.

6. Adapted from Richard F. Stolz, "Ah, To Be Strategic," *Human Resource Executive,* November 2003, 1, 20–27.

7. Adapted from Tom Starner, "Processing a Turnaround," *Human Resource Executive,* May 16, 2004, 1, 16–23.

8. This section draws substantially from Anne Freedman, "Dealing with Trouble," *Human Resource Executive,* August 2004, 1, 22–28.

9. Adapted from Freedman, "Dealing with Trouble."

Chapter 11

1. Susan J. Wells, "From HR to the Top," *HR Magazine,* June 2003.

2. The suggestions in this section are drawn from the following sources: Susan J. Wells, "From HR to the Top," *HR Magazine,* June 2003; Magda Du Preez and Eugene Buccini, "Strategies for Being Seen and Heard at the Executive Table," SHRM white paper, Society for Human Resource Management, Alexandria, VA, March 2004; and Lin Grensing-Pophal, "Getting a 'Seat at the Table'—What Does It Really Take?" SHRM white paper, Society for Human Resource Management, Alexandria, VA, August 2000.

3. Adapted from Susan J. Wells, "Five Who Have Made It," *HR Magazine,* June 2003.

Glossary

AFFILIATIVE MANAGER Per David McClelland and David Burnham, a manager who is more interested in being liked than in having and using power to get the job done.

ANTITHESIS A rhetorical device that places a sentence or one of its parts in opposition to another in order to capture attention or to evoke a strong response.

CENTER OF INFLUENCE An individual having the power to influence those around him or her.

COALITION A temporary alliance of separate entities or individuals who join together to seek a common purpose. See also *natural coalition* and *single-issue coalition.*

CREDIBILITY The quality of inspiring belief in and acknowledgment of one's expertise, abilities, and knowledge.

CURRENCIES OF EXCHANGE Per Allan Cohen and David Bradford, the coinage of influence; resources that can be offered to a potential ally in exchange for cooperation.

EMPATHY The ability to identify with or vicariously experience the thoughts or feelings of others.

FRAME A mental window through which a person or organization views reality or a particular problem.

INFLUENCE The mechanism through which people use power to change behavior or attitudes. Unlike power, influence can produce an effect without the apparent exertion of force, compulsion, or direct command.

INFLUENCE NETWORK A network of individuals through which influence is made or enforced. In this network, some individuals have greater influence than others.

INFLUENCERS   Individuals who participate indirectly in the decision-making process. They provide advice and information to key stakeholders and decision makers.

INSTITUTIONAL MANAGER   Per David McClelland and David Burnham, a manager who deploys power in the service of the organization and not in the service of personal goals.

LAW OF RECIPROCITY   A general rule that demands that every favor must someday be repaid.

MANIPULATION   Per Allan Cohen and David Bradford, actions taken to achieve influence that would be rendered less effective if the other party knew the manipulator's actual intentions.

METAPHOR   An imaginative way of describing something as something else—for example, "Business is war." When a metaphor shapes someone's viewpoint, it becomes an *organizing metaphor.*

NATURAL COALITION   A coalition of allies who share a broad range of common interests.

OPINION LEADER   See *center of influence.*

ORGANIZING METAPHOR   An overarching worldview that shapes a person's everyday actions—for example, "Business is war." See also *metaphor.*

PARALLEL STRUCTURE   A rhetorical device that uses sentence elements that are alike in both function and construction—for example, "We will work hard. We will work smart. We will not tire or fail."

PERSONAL POWER   Power that is a function of one or many qualities: ideas, expertise, accomplishments, charisma, communication skill, and trustworthiness.

PERSONAL POWER MANAGER   Per scholars David McClelland and David Burnham, a manager whose personal need for power exceeds his need to be liked. This manager seeks power for himself and for people on his team in order to get the job done. Subordinates like this kind of boss and often become very loyal because the boss makes them feel strong. On the negative side, this manager is a power aggrandizer and turf builder and not a good institution builder.

PERSUASION   A process through which one can change or reinforce the attitudes, opinions, or behaviors of others.

POWER   The potential to allocate resources and to make and enforce decisions.

POWER OF POSITION   The power or authority associated with one's formal position in an organization.

RELATIONAL POWER   Informal power that emerges from one's relationships with others.

RHETORICAL QUESTION   A question asked for the sole purpose of producing an effect on the audience. The speaker does not expect the question to be answered—least of all by the audience.

SINGLE-ISSUE COALITION   A coalition of parties that differ on other issues but unite to support or block a single issue (often for different reasons).

SOCIAL NETWORK   An invisible web of collaborative relationships that do not appear on a company's formal organizational chart or reporting hierarchy.

SPHERE OF INFLUENCE   The domain in which a person can effectively exert influence.

TRIAD   A rhetorical device that uses a list of three items.

For Further Reading

Books

Barnes, B. Kim. *Exercising Influence: A Guide for Making Things Happen at Work, at Home, and in Your Community.* Berkeley, CA: Barnes & Conti, 2000. The author draws on her experience as an organizational consultant to explain how you can employ influence to accomplish more in the three major arenas of life: work, home, and community. One interesting feature is the author's chapter on influence planning.

Brockbank, Wayne, and Dave Ulrich. *Competencies for the New HR.* Alexandria, VA: Society for Human Resource Management, Michigan Business School, and Global Consulting Alliance, 2003. The authors define new competency domains for HR professionals, including strategic contribution, personal credibility, HR delivery, business knowledge, and HR technology. They also provide guidelines for developing these competency domains. For example, to strengthen personal credibility—an essential ingredient in your use of power, influence, and persuasion— you need to build a track record of results, cultivate networks of effective relationships, and burnish your communication skills.

Cohen, Allan R., and David L. Bradford. *Influence Without Authority.* New York: John Wiley & Sons, 1989. Written by two outstanding business scholars, this book addresses a problem faced by a growing number of managers: how to lead when they are thrust into positions of responsibility with no corresponding authority. The authors describe how to obtain the cooperation of managers who control resources and information but who are not obliged to cooperate. Points in the book are nicely illustrated with case examples.

Cross, Rob, and Andrew Parker. *The Hidden Power of Social Networks: Understanding How Work Really Gets Done in Organizations.* Boston: Harvard Business School Press, 2004. The authors define invisible social networks, explain the value they generate, and provide suggestions for leveraging their power. You'll find a wealth of suggestions for identifying the social networks in your organization, as well as strengthening existing ones and creating new ones.

Dobson, Michael, and Deborah Singer Dobson. *Managing Up: 59 Ways to Build a Career-Advancing Relationship with Your Boss.* New York: AMACOM, 2000. The quality of the relationship you cultivate with your boss can strongly determine how much power, influence, and persuasiveness you acquire. The authors provide potent tips for creating a positive, effective bond with your supervisor—whether you report to an HR manager or executive or to your company's CEO.

Downey, Diane. *Assimilating New Leaders: The Key to Executive Retention.* New York: AMACOM, 2001. Assimilating new leaders is one of the most effective ways HR practitioners can exercise and enhance their power and influence in an organization. This author provides a compelling business case for focusing on new leader assimilation, and an innovative set of tools and approaches that will help you enable your organization to integrate and retain top executives.

Getting People on Board. The Results-Driven Manager Series. Boston: Harvard Business School Press, 2005. This volume in the Results-Driven Manager series provides a variety of articles on influencing and motivating others. Topics include leading without formal authority, overcoming resistance to your ideas, and communicating effectively to exert influence and persuade (such as framing issues your way).

Kotter, John P. *Power and Influence.* Boston: Harvard Business School Press, 1985. In the complex world of work, things no longer get done simply because someone issues an order and someone else follows it. Most of us work in socially intricate organizations where we need the help not only of subordinates but also of colleagues, superiors, and outsiders to accomplish our goals. This often leaves us facing a "power gap" because we must depend on people over whom we have little or no explicit control. This book is about how to bridge that gap: how to exercise power and influence to get things done through others when your responsibilities exceed your formal authority. Kotter explains how to develop sufficient resources of unofficial power and influence to achieve goals, steer clear of conflicts, foster creative team behavior, and gain the cooperation and support you need from subordinates, coworkers, and superiors—even people outside your department or organization. He also shows how you can avoid the twin traps of naiveté and cynicism when dealing with power relationships, and how to use power without abusing it.

Leavitt, Harold J. *Top Down: Why Hierarchies Are Here to Stay and How to Manage Them More Effectively.* Boston: Harvard Business School Press, 2004. Corporate hierarchies satisfy important needs—which is why they remain the most workable and effective structures humans have invented for performing large, complex tasks. Leavitt shows how managers can maneuver within their company's hierarchy to build networks of influence, empower themselves and others, and motivate other people to do what they want—and need—them to do in order to fulfill their responsibilities.

Ludwig, Arnold D. *King of the Mountain: The Nature of Political Leadership.* Louisville: University of Kentucky Press, 2002. In this book, emeritus professor of psychiatry Arnold Ludwig reports the results of his study of 377 world leaders and his thoughts about why people seek to rule (i.e., why they seek power). One of his observations is that power seekers are very similar to alpha male primates, who are driven to establish themselves as the dominant members of their groups. Readers will enjoy the author's analysis of Idi Amin, Tony Blair, William Churchill, Ronald Reagan, and others, and the factors that drove them to seek power.

Mills, Harry. *Artful Persuasion: How to Command Attention, Change Minds, and Influence People.* New York: AMACOM, 2000. Mills makes it clear that anyone can learn to be a skilled persuader. In this book, he explores the psychology behind persuasion and reveals how the most successful persuaders work their magic. Exploring both the conscious and unconscious forces at play, Mills provides practical guidelines for tackling the toughest challenges of persuasion, such as winning over hostile audiences, connecting emotionally with audiences, and getting your audiences to persuade themselves to support your ideas.

Pfeffer, Jeffrey. *Managing with Power: Politics and Influence in Organizations.* Boston: Harvard Business School Press, 1992. Pfeffer presents power as the means by which managers influence others' behavior, change the course of events in their organizations, overcome resistance, and motivate people to take action—in other words, exert strong leadership. The author provides an in-depth and fascinating look at the role of power and influence in organizations, revealing how you gain power and use it to get things done. Anyone, Pfeffer maintains, can cultivate an awareness of how power works, increase his or her own influence, and learn how others gain theirs.

Presentations That Persuade and Motivate. The Results-Driven Manager Series. Boston: Harvard Business School Press, 2004. This volume in the Results-Driven Manager series offers valuable selections on the many aspects of delivering a compelling presentation. You'll find selections on preparation (such as choosing the right structure for your speech and managing stage fright), delivery (including using visuals and handling questions), and use of tools and techniques (such as using your physical presence to engender trust in your audience).

Watkins, Michael. *The First 90 Days: Critical Success Strategies for New Leaders at All Levels.* Boston: Harvard Business School Press, 2003. The author provides a road map for taking charge quickly and effectively during critical career transitions, whether you're a first-time HR manager or a senior executive. You'll find proven strategies that dramatically shorten the time it takes to reach what Watkins calls the "breakeven point": the point at which your organization needs you as much as you need the job. Strategies include negotiating a productive working relationship with your boss, securing early wins that establish credibility, and building your team and connecting with influential support coalitions.

Notes and Articles

Buss, Dale. "Corporate Compasses." *HR Magazine,* June 2004. Buss explains the increasing importance of ethics officers in organizations, and clarifies HR professionals' role in upholding ethical behavior in their companies. With incidents of unethical use of power on the upswing in corporations, no HR professional can afford not to educate himself or herself on how to prevent malfeasance.

Cialdini, Robert B. "Harnessing the Science of Persuasion." *Harvard Business Review,* OnPoint Enhanced Edition, October 2001, 72–79. Cialdini shines the spotlight on persuasion triggers—the subconscious mental shortcuts people take to make decisions when they're pressed for time, fatigued, or distracted. Drawing from the behavioral sciences, Cialdini explores the following triggers: liking (people like those who like them), reciprocity (people repay favors in kind), social proof (people follow the lead of others like themselves), consistency (people align with clear commitments), authority (people defer to experts), and scarcity (people want more of what they have less of).

Claus, Lisbeth, and Jessica Collison. *The Maturing Profession of Human Resources in the United States of America Survey Report.* Alexandria, VA: Society for Human Resource Management, January 2004. This research report provides information related to HR professionals' power and influence—including definitions of what constitutes credibility and professionalism, why these are increasingly important to today's HR practitioner, and what current reporting relationships suggest about HR professionals' influence in their organizations.

Conger, Jay A. "The Necessary Art of Persuasion." *Harvard Business Review,* OnPoint Enhanced Edition, May–June 1998, 84–94. This article defines and explains the four essential elements of persuasion. Business today is run largely by teams and populated by authority-averse baby boomers and generation Xers. That makes persuasion more important than ever as a managerial tool. But contrary to popular belief, asserts author Jay Conger (director of the Leadership Institute of the University of Southern California's Marshall Business School), persuasion is not the same as selling an idea or convincing opponents to see things your way. Instead, it is a process of learning from others and negotiating a shared solution. To that end, persuasion consists of these essential elements: establishing credibility, framing to find common ground, providing vivid evidence, and connecting emotionally. Persuasion can be a force for enormous good in an organization, but people must understand it for what it is: an often painstaking process that requires insight, planning, and compromise.

Du Preez, Magda, and Eugene Buccini. "Strategies for Being Seen and Heard at the Executive Table." SHRM white paper, Society for Human Resource Management, Alexandria, VA, March 2004. The authors provide suggestions for exerting influence during strategic decision making at your company—including learning as much as you can about your organization's business, demonstrating your willingness to take risks and make hard decisions, earning a reputation for trustworthiness, understanding obstacles to your company's achievement of its strategy, and forging enabling alliances with other executives.

Freedman, Anne. "Dealing with Trouble: The Story of the Rise and Fall at AOL of Former HR Leader Gregory S. Horton." *Human Resource Executive,* August 2004, 1, 22–28. This case study offers valuable lessons for anyone seeking ways to prevent the unethical use of power, influence, and persuasion.

Hattersley, Michael. "Persuasion." Note 9-392-012. Boston: Harvard Business School Publishing, September 19, 1991. This note examines the principles that apply in any persuasive business situation. It describes how to analyze the goals and audience, how to devise a persuasive message, and how to execute a persuasive strategy in writing, presentations, and larger corporate communication tasks.

Joseph, Joshua, and Evren Esen. *2003 Business Ethics Survey.* Alexandria, VA: SHRM/Ethics Resource Center, April 2003. This research report assesses numerous aspects of business ethics, including the forces behind unethical use of power and influence and the various forms in which such conduct manifests itself.

Leonard, Bill. "Straight Talk." *HR Magazine,* January 2002. Leonard offers advice on ways to influence your company's strategic direction and persuade others to support your strategic initiatives. Suggestions include familiarizing yourself with advances in information technology and identifying ways to leverage them—for example, by providing just-in-time training. You'll also need a thorough understanding of your company's business and its strategic plan, as well as an ability to show how HR can help implement that plan.

Long-Lingo, Elizabeth, and Kathleen McGinn. "Power and Influence: Achieving Your Objectives in Organizations." Note 9-801-425. Boston: Harvard Business School Publishing, April 4, 2002. Power, as described in this Harvard Business School class note, is the potential to mobilize energy. This rather neutral definition does not address the issues of how to exercise power or to what ends. The answers to these questions determine the ultimate value of an individual's power. This note is written to help you analyze the social system in which your power exists and your influence will be used. Following the guidelines presented, a careful analysis of the social system in which an individual operates and an assessment of that individual's desires and objectives within the social system may help maximize the development of power and the effective use of influence.

Marton, Betty A. "Mastering the Art of Persuasion." *Harvard Management Communication Letter,* July 2000, 3–5. Marton surveys the experts' thinking on the subject of persuasion, listing dos and don'ts for aspiring as well as seasoned persuaders—for example, do develop empathy so that you can accurately perceive how others feel, and do become an effective team builder. You'll learn how to build a coalition of support so that you know whom to go to when you need to make a pitch. But don't take a strong position at the start of your persuasion effort—you'll only give potential resisters something to fight against. And don't confuse argument with persuasion. Arguing your position is only one part of effective persuasion. You'll also need to rely on effective communication, empathy, and emotional connection with your audiences.

McClelland, David C., and David H. Burnham. "Power Is the Great Motivator." *Harvard Business Review,* January 2003, 3–11. To motivate others, managers must be motivated themselves. The key issue here is the source of the motivation—the way the manager defines success. Some equate success with personal achievement; others see success as being liked by others. To succeed in a complex organization, a manager needs to have a power motivation, which is not a dictatorial impulse but rather the desire to have an impact, to be strong and influential. This power, according to the authors, must be disciplined and channeled in ways that benefit the organization and not the manager herself.

Mollica, Kelly. "Perceptions of Fairness." *HR Magazine,* June 2004. In exerting your power, influence, and persuasion skills with direct reports, you won't get far unless they perceive you as fair. To that end, Mollica offers strategies for earning a reputation for fairness—including explaining the reasoning behind your decisions, demonstrating genuine interest in your

people's success, basing decisions on accurate information, seeking outside opinions before making decisions, treating people with consistency,
giving employees a voice in decisions that affect them, and being willing
to change your mind if new information suggests doing so.

Roberts, Bill. "Side by Side." *HR Magazine,* March 2004. HR professionals
further build their ability to exert influence by cultivating positive relationships with other members of the executive team. In this article,
Roberts focuses on the importance of a good relationship between a
company's HR leader and its chief information officer. Today, much of
an HR executive's success is tied to technology-enabled HR processes,
which means that your relationship with your firm's CIO is crucial to
getting the results that will satisfy your CEO. Keys to a good relationship
with the CIO include a shared vision for your company, management
expertise outside information technology and HR, and frequent interaction and conversation about the company's goals.

Simpson, Liz. "Get Around Resistance and Win Over the Other Side." *Harvard Management Communication Letter,* April 2003, 3–5. Simpson focuses
on the crucial obstacle that most persuaders encounter numerous times:
opposition to their ideas. She explains how to step into your opponent's
shoes by discerning the concerns and emotions fueling the resistance.
By listening closely, you demonstrate that you're taking the resister's
interests to heart and earning his or her trust. The resister then becomes
more open to seeing things from your perspective. In addition to listening, make your verbal and nonverbal messages consistent and present
your resister's point of view before your own.

Starner, Tom. "Processing a Turnaround." *Human Resource Executive,* May
16, 2004, 1, 16–23. During tough times—such as turnaround of a troubled company—the way you extend your power, influence, and persuasion skills becomes more important than ever. This article describes how
one HR executive used her skills to help her company reverse an alarm-
ing downward slide—including developing and winning support for
potent initiatives.

Stolz, Richard F. "Ah, To Be Strategic." *Human Resource Executive,* November 2003, 1, 20–27. The author describes how one HR executive
exerted his power, influence, and persuasion to manage the HR function strategically. His keys to success include viewing HR as a business
tasked with meeting the needs of "customers" within the larger enterprise, providing performance data to other divisions, demonstrating the
bottom-line impact of HR initiatives, and "not being afraid to fail."

Watkins, Michael D. "The Power to Persuade." Note 9-800-323. Boston:
Harvard Business School Publishing, July 2000. Watkins explains how to

master core persuasion tasks. For example, to map the influence landscape, identify who you need to persuade; decide who your supporters, opponents, and "persuadables" are; assess their interests and the reasons for any resistance; and figure out what they see as their alternatives to the change you're proposing. To shape perceptions of interests, introduce rewards for desired behavior and impose disincentives for undesired behavior. Also frame your pitch deliberately—for example, by heightening concerns about loss or risk or linking the proposed change to your audience's core values. To gain acceptance for tough decisions, create a fair process by which your audience feels you've taken their concerns and ideas into account.

Wells, Susan J. "Five Who Have Made It." *HR Magazine,* June 2003. Wells provides case studies of five HR professionals who have advanced into the top executive echelons in their organizations. Each case study delineates the person's current responsibilities, path to the top, ways in which his or her HR background helped, perceptions of HR among the topmost executives in his or her organization, and career advice for colleagues.

Wells, Susan J. "From HR to the Top." *HR Magazine,* June 2003. The author suggests strategies for enhancing your power, influence, and persuasion skills so as to further your career. Advice includes accumulating cross-functional experience, cultivating a positive relationship with your company's chief financial officer (who is likely facing increasing pressure to show how the company's people assets are being managed), and developing a defensible point of view of your company's entire business.

Williams, Gary A., and Robert B. Miller. "Change the Way You Persuade." *Harvard Business Review,* OnPoint Enhanced Edition, May 2002, 3–11. The authors urge persuaders to tailor their efforts to their audience members' decision-making styles. Different individuals, they maintain, have different preferences for deciding whether to accept an idea. Each wants certain kinds of information at specific steps in the decision-making process. There are five styles that most persuaders will likely encounter in the workplace:

- Charismatic: easily enthralled but bases final decisions on balanced information
- Thinker: needs extensive detail
- Skeptic: challenges every data point
- Follower: relies on her own or others' past decisions
- Controller: implements only his own ideas

For each style, the authors lay out corresponding strategies and examples of how to implement them.

Additional Titles from the Society for Human Resource Management (SHRM)®

Carrig, Ken, and Patrick M. Wright. *Building Profit through Building People: Making Your Workforce the Strongest Link in the Value-Profit Chain*

Collier, T. O., Jr. *Supervisor's Guide to Labor Relations*

Cook, Mary, and Scott Gildner. *Outsourcing Human Resources Functions: How, Why, When, and When Not to Contract for HR Services*

Gardenswartz, Lee, and Anita Rowe. *Diverse Teams at Work*

Grensing-Pophal, Lin, SPHR. *Human Resource Essentials: Your Guide to Starting and Running the HR Function*

Landry, R.J. *The Comprehensive, All-in-One HR Operating Guide.* 539 ready-to-adapt human resources policies, practices, letters, memos, forms . . . and more.

HR Source Book Series

Bliss, Wendy, JD, SPHR, and Gene Thornton, Esq., PHR. *Employment Termination Source Book*

Deblieux, Mike. *Performance Appraisal Source Book*

Fyock, Cathy, CSP, SPHR. *Hiring Source Book*

Hubbartt, William S., SPHR, CCP. *HIPAA Privacy Source Book*

Lambert, Jonamay, M.A. and Selma Myers, M.A. *Trainer's Diversity Source Book*

Practical HR Series

Bliss, Wendy, JD, SPHR. *Legal, Effective References: How to Give and Get Them*

Oppenheimer, Amy, JD, and Craig Pratt, MSW, SPHR. *Investigating Workplace Harassment: How to Be Fair, Thorough, and Legal*

Phillips, Jack J., PhD and Patricia Pulliam Phillips, PhD. *Proving the Value of HR: How and Why to Measure ROI*

Shaw, Seyfarth, LLP. *Understanding the Federal Wage & Hour Laws: What Employers Must Know about FLSA and its Overtime Regulations*

How to Order from SHRM

SHRM offers a member discount on all books that it publishes or sells. To order this or any other book published by the Society, contact the SHRM-Store.®

Online: www.shrm.org/shrmstore

Phone: 1-800-444-5006 (option #1); or 770-442-8633 (ext. 362); or tdd 703-548-6999

Fax: 770-442-9742

Mail: SHRM Distribution Center, P.O. Box 930132, Atlanta, GA 31193-0132, USA

Index

About the Subject Adviser

DR. KATHLEEN KELLEY REARDON, Professor of Management and Organization in the University of Southern California Marshall School of Business, is a leading authority on persuasion, negotiation, and politics in the workplace. She is author of seven books and numerous articles published in leading communication and business journals, including the *Harvard Business Review.* Her book *The Secret Handshake: Mastering the Politics of the Business Inner Circle,* released in early 2001 (Doubleday), rapidly became a business best seller in the United States. Dr. Reardon's most recent books include *The Skilled Negotiator* (JosseyBass), *On Becoming a Skilled Negotiator* (Wiley), and *It's All Politics* (Currency/Doubleday).

Dr. Reardon has served on the prestigious *Harvard Business Review* McKinsey Award Panel and the editorial boards of several academic journals. She was elected to the board of the International Communication Association and the founding advisory board of First Star, an organization devoted to promoting the rights of children. In 2004 she was designated the first Distinguished Research Scholar of The Irish Management Institute.

Dr. Reardon is a Phi Beta Kappa graduate of the University of Connecticut (BA) and received her MA and PhD summa cum laude and with distinction from the University of Massachusetts at Amherst.

About the Series Adviser

WENDY BLISS, JD, SPHR, has experience as a human resource executive, attorney, senior editor, and professional speaker. Since 1994, she has provided human resource consulting, corporate training, and coaching services nationally through her Colorado Springs–based consulting firm, Bliss & Associates.

Ms. Bliss is the author of *Legal, Effective References: How to Give and Get Them* (Society of Human Resource Management, 2001) and was a contributor to *Human Resource Essentials* (Society for Human Resource Management, 2002). She has published numerous articles in magazines and periodicals, including *HR Magazine, Employment Management Today, HR Matters,* and the *Denver University Law Review.*

Ms. Bliss has a Juris Doctor degree from the University of Denver College of Law and has been certified as a Senior Professional in Human Resources (SPHR) by the Human Resource Certification Institute. Since 1999, she has conducted human resource certificate programs for the Society for Human Resource Management. Previously, she was an adjunct faculty member at the University of Colorado at Colorado Springs and at the University of Phoenix, where she taught graduate and undergraduate courses in human resource management, employment law, organizational behavior, and business communications. Additionally, Ms. Bliss has served on the board of directors for several professional associations and nonprofit organizations and was a president of the National Board of Governors for the Society for Human Resource Management's Consultants Forum.

National media, including *ABC News, Time* magazine, the *New York Times,* the Associated Press, the *Washington Post,* USAToday.com, and *HR Magazine,* have looked to Ms. Bliss for expert opinions on workplace issues.

About the Writers

LAUREN KELLER JOHNSON has contributed to several volumes in the Business Literacy for Human Resource Professionals series. Based in Harvard, Massachusetts, Ms. Keller Johnson writes for numerous business publications. Her work has appeared in the *Harvard Business Review* OnPoint Series, *Harvard Management Update* newsletter, *Contingent Workforce Strategies* magazine, *Sloan Management Review,* the *Balanced Scorecard Report,* and *Supply Chain Strategy* newsletter. She has ghostwritten several books and online training modules for managers. She has a master's degree in technical and professional writing from Northeastern University.

RICHARD LUECKE is the writer of several books in the Harvard Business Essentials series. Based in Salem, Massachusetts, Mr. Luecke has authored or developed more than thirty books and dozens of articles on a wide range of business subjects. He has an MBA from the University of St. Thomas.

About the Society for Human Resource Management

The Society for Human Resource Management (SHRM) is the world's largest association devoted to human resource management. Representing more than 170,000 individual members, the Society's mission is to serve the needs of HR professionals by providing the most essential and comprehensive resources available. As an influential voice, the Society's mission is also to advance the human resource profession to ensure that HR is recognized as an essential partner in developing and executing organizational strategy. Visit SHRM Online at www.shrm.org.

The Results-Driven Manager

The Results-Driven Manager series collects timely articles from Harvard Management Update and Harvard Management Communication Letter to help senior to middle managers sharpen their skills, increase their effectiveness, and gain a competitive edge. Presented in a concise, accessible format to save managers valuable time, these books offer authoritative insights and techniques for improving job performance and achieving immediate results.

These books are priced at $14.95 U.S.
Price subject to change.

How to Order

Harvard Business School Press publications are available worldwide from your local bookseller or online retailer.

You can also call

1-800-668-6780

Our product consultants are available to help you
8:00 a.m.–6:00 p.m., Monday–Friday, Eastern Time.
Outside the U.S. and Canada, call: 617-783-7450
Please call about special discounts for quantities greater than ten.

You can order online at

www.HBSPress.org